EVERYDAY PRAYERS

— FOR —

FAITH

Finding Confidence in God No Matter What

ERIN H. WARREN

WHITAKER
HOUSE

EVERYDAY PRAYERS FOR FAITH
Finding Confidence in God No Matter What

erinhwarren.com
www.instagram.com/erinhwarren

ISBN: 979-8-88769-120-6
eBook ISBN: 979-8-88769-121-3
Printed in Colombia
© 2024 by Erin H. Warren

Whitaker House
1030 Hunt Valley Circle
New Kensington, PA 15068
www.whitakerhouse.com

Library of Congress Control Number: 2023946066

1 2 3 4 5 6 7 8 9 10 11 ⨆⨆ 31 30 29 28 27 26 25 24

DEDICATION

To Stacey, Amy, and Tanya:

Your faith sharpens my faith. Thank you for being the kind of friends who would tear the roof off to get me to Jesus. I love you so much, EATS!

CONTENTS

FOREWORD

I'm the kind of girl who falls often. I've twisted my ankle so many times in my lifetime that it's become a joke in my family. If there's a hole within walking distance, I will fall into it. I have twisted my ankle while standing still (I'm not kidding), while walking on a firm sidewalk, and, most notably, while sitting at a table playing an intense game of Scrabble with my family. That one landed me in the office of an orthopedist, who promptly told me that if I didn't stop abusing my ankles this way, I would eventually need surgery. When my husband and I are walking into a building, or approaching any kind of uneven surface, he will lift my hand up as we approach a step...as if this act will somehow tell my brain that my foot needs to act. It's his way of trying to help.

The threat of surgery, and my intense desire to avoid it, caused me to begin to look down at the ground when I walk, especially on uneven surfaces. I once walked through my in-laws' backyard—a particularly uneven space—and ran into a tree because I was too busy looking at where I was placing my feet. Luckily, it was a branch and not the trunk, but still, I ran into a tree.

I know my story is funny, and I told it intentionally to make you laugh. (I can take you laughing at me. It's okay.) But I hope it also serves to illustrate a deeper truth.

We all desire sure footing. Something to hold onto, or some kind of control when it feels like we're falling. I look down when I walk in an effort to protect myself. If I don't, I can't see potential dangers, like holes or uneven ground, that could hurt me. I look to the Word of God and to God Himself to protect me from the bumpy surprises of life. If I don't, I won't understand or be able to withstand when things don't go as I planned.

That's called faith.

There are all kinds of weird and mystical definitions for the word *faith*. I've often heard the word used in the middle of high school sports games...even college or pro games...to muster some kind of deep feeling that propels an athlete forward in spite of pain, discouragement, or loss. "Dig deep! Have faith!" I've probably screamed some version of those words myself watching my own kids play ball.

Some definitions of faith point to belief in a power outside of ourselves. Other definitions suggest a power from within. Still others point toward a religious experience or truth. The definitions of faith are varied but they all have one element in common: they're based on something that can't be seen.

The Bible speaks to this in the book of Hebrews: *"Now faith is the reality of what is hoped for, the proof of what is not seen"* (Hebrews 11:1 csb). In his paraphrase Bible, *The Message*, Eugene Peterson describes faith this way: *"The fundamental fact of existence is that this trust in God, this faith, is the firm foundation under everything that makes life worth living. It's our handle on what we can't see"* (Hebrews 11:1 msg).

Something to hold on to when nothing makes sense...or maybe something that makes sense of what appears on the surface to be senseless. That's how I understand faith. Either way, it's firm footing when the world we live in feels full of twist-your-ankle terrain. And I need all of that that I can get.

Yes, there are many definitions of faith, but there's only one definition that gives the believer that kind of surety, and it doesn't come from within us. It isn't mystical, or something we can muster from our own strength. It comes from knowing God and through a relationship with His Son, Jesus. Over the next thirty days, my friend Erin Warren is going to take you on a journey through that kind of faith. In the end, you'll believe in the faithfulness of the God you've put your faith in. There's no better person I can think of to take you on this trip, and no better time than right now to take it. Erin and her family have endured all kinds of potholes, detours, and experiences that made the world around them seem foggy instead of clear. They've tripped and stumbled over uneven ground. But instead of allowing those struggles to turn them away from God, they have grabbed on to the handle of His Word, which has given them a handle on the world they live in. They live in faith.

You can too.

Join Erin as she leads you into a study of what true, biblical faith really is. Explore with her the God who inspired these words:

Because of the LORD's great love we are not consumed, for his compassions never fail. They are new every morning; great is your faithfulness. —Lamentations 3:22–23 NIV

Together,

Brooke McGlothlin
Founder, Million Praying Moms

Note:

This devotional uses Million Praying Moms'
"Think, Pray, Praise" method of daily prayer.
If you are not familiar with this prayer practice, please visit:

www.millionprayingmoms.com/
the-think-pray-praise-method-of-daily-prayer

INTRODUCTION

FAITH IN A FAITHFUL GOD

My family and I were enjoying a much-needed day of fun at a local theme park. We drove the race cars and rode the carousel. We savored ice cream and Florida's beautiful winter weather. It was glorious. We ventured to the pioneer area to explore the caves and forts. There we began an unsteady walk across a barrel bridge. We laughed as we struggled to keep our balance while the barrels bobbed and sent us up, down, and sideways. While I laughed, I also knew that the bridge was a metaphor for my life.

We were coming off of four years of living in crisis and survival mode on an unsteady path. I felt tossed to and fro by circumstances that were out of my control, and I desperately wanted to be back on solid ground.

Our unsteady journey began when my husband Kris experienced some medical problems. Various doctors chased symptoms and ran tests. Kris tried different medications but nothing worked. After about six months of searching, he ended up in the hospital. We thought he would be there a few hours, but hours turned into days. Doctors ran test after test, and while they began to rule out some of the big scary things, they still didn't know what was wrong with Kris. Finally, after spending five days in the hospital, Kris was diagnosed with an autoimmune disease, a chronic illness that he would have the rest of his life. My faith began to waver.

Kris was really sick, and an army of friends and family stepped in to support us. But every time someone said, "God is faithful" to me, something in my stomach turned. I kept thinking, *My husband will most likely never be healed, so what's faithful about that?*

Don't get me wrong—it wasn't that I didn't *believe* God could heal him. It's that I now lived with this tension of living in a broken world with broken bodies where healing does not always happen. I had to face the reality that God may *not* heal, no matter how much I prayed. No matter how much I wanted it. The reality of living this side of heaven is that we do not always get the outcome we desire.

I probably don't have to tell you that. My guess is that you too have faced your share of disappointments in life. Maybe you have also pondered God's faithfulness in all of it. Is He still faithful when life's twists and turns don't go as we had planned? Can I still put my faith in God when my circumstances are not what I had hoped?

I myself am guilty of saying "God is faithful" a thousand times—when someone got the job, the guy, the baby, or the win, when surgery went well, or when things went my way. That is our go-to phrase. But it wasn't until I was faced with my own crisis that I began to question that very truth.

The problem with saying "God is faithful" in the face of good, earthly circumstances is that it opens up some questions. Does that mean God is not faithful to the one whose husband died? Is God not faithful to the one who never had the baby? Is God not faithful to the one who never got the promotion? Is God not faithful to the one who did not see the healing or the outcome they desired? Tying His faithfulness to the good, earthly outcomes of our story causes us to question the very character of God. And when we do that, we begin to question our faith in our faithful God.

God is faithful, and God doesn't change. I knew that. So I started wondering if I had misunderstood the meaning of His faithfulness.

If His faithfulness is not tied to the outcomes of my earthly circumstances, what then is His faithfulness? That's when I began my journey of wrestling, and what He revealed in that time completely changed the way I see God and His faithfulness.

TRUE FAITHFULNESS

One of the definitions of *faithful* is "firm in adherence to promises."[1] God's faithfulness is that He keeps His promises. Which begs the question: What, then, does God promise us? When I searched for His promises in Scripture, God began to do a great work in my life. It was during this time that God gripped my heart with a passion for His Word. I began reading Scripture as I never had before—with a lens focused on the character of God and His promises.

At first, I was disappointed to learn that His promises are not wealth, health, relationships, and children. I wanted that to be true, but that's not His promise to us. I discovered instead that His faithfulness and His promises are greater and of greater worth than anything He could give us here on earth. In 2 Peter 1:4, Peter calls the promises of God *"precious"* and *"very great."* They are of utmost value and wonderfully magnificent. Knowing God's promises helps us ward off the temptation of sin. It helps us become more like Jesus, so that we literally share in the very likeness and character of God.

And it's all ours through the blood of Jesus Christ.

LET'S FEAST

As I read Scripture looking for the promises of God, I began to see just how great and amazing and awesome our God is. I am a Bible teacher at heart, and I have fallen in love with God's Word.

Over the next thirty days, I want to journey with you through the promises of our faithful God. All of these promises are yours to hold. *"In* [Jesus] *it is always Yes. For all the promises of God find their Yes in him"* (2 Corinthians 1:19–20).

---

1. *Merriam-Webster Dictionary*, s.v. "Faithful," www.merriam-webster.com/dictionary/faithful.

We can put our faith in our faithful God. Faith is assurance and trust—a firm belief that God is who He says He is. I know firsthand that this life brings heartache and fear and trouble and questions. But I also know that greater is He who is within me than he who is in the world. (See 1 John 4:4.) Our circumstances may tempt us to doubt the faithfulness of God. Satan wants us to believe that God is holding out on us. Satan wants us to forget the promises of God and wants us to be confused about who God is. But Satan *"is a liar and the father of lies"* (John 8:44). He comes to steal, kill, and destroy. (See John 10:10.)

Christ came so that we may experience the abundance that awaits us in the character and promises of God. We can trust Him. *"Trust in the Lord, and do good; dwell in the land and befriend faithfulness"* (Psalm 37:3). The Hebrew word for *befriend* can also be translated "feed on faithfulness." We are called to trust Him and feast on His abundant faithfulness.

Arm yourself with the knowledge of His promises. As you read through these promises, I highly encourage you to look up the additional verses. His Word is a shield over your heart and mind. These promises are a sword with which you can fight when you are tempted to believe God is not faithful. Because God *is* faithful, you can put your full faith and confidence in Him.

When we walked across that barrel bridge in January 2020, I was hopeful about the year to come, but I had no idea that the years of crisis were only going to continue. As I bobbed along behind my kids, my youngest, who was five at the time, threw his arms out, leapt the final three feet of the bridge, and exclaimed, "I. TRUST. IN. GOD!" for the entire park to hear. After he landed on the solid sidewalk beyond the bridge, he turned back and confidently said, "Yep. Totally trusted in God."

Sweet friend, I do not know what unsteady journey you are traversing right now, but I do know this: Our God is faithful, and you can trust Him. You can put your confidence in Him even though life may be tossing you to and fro. His promises are a firm foundation that will carry you through.

As I write this, my family is walking through yet another health crisis, but God's promises are far richer, far greater, and far more valuable than any outcome here on earth. Therefore, *"Let us hold unswervingly to the hope we profess, for he who promised is faithful"* (Hebrews 10:23 NIV).

I pray that over these next thirty days, God will meet you in the pages of His Word, and your faith will be strengthened by His very precious and abundant promises.

DAY 1

GOD IS FAITHFUL TO SAVE

*If you confess with your mouth that Jesus is Lord
and believe in your heart that God raised him from the dead,
you will be saved.*
—Romans 10:9

I was maybe five or six years old when I said *the prayer*. My memory isn't perfect, but I remember sitting on my daddy's knee at our dining room table and praying to receive Jesus as my Savior. And with that decision, the whole trajectory of my life was changed. No, I didn't fully understand the weight of my words. I would spend the next several decades learning what it means to put my faith in Jesus. Truthfully, I am still learning, but I was set on a course that day.

Over the years, I've heard many people say that little children are too young to understand what it means to accept Jesus as their Savior. But my mom encouraged me in spite of their doubts. She said, "I never wanted to discount what God might be doing in the hearts of my children." And I'm so thankful she continued to encourage me in my faith, because our God is faithful to save.

The book of Romans is one of the most comprehensive and complete gospel explanations in Scripture. The church in Rome was divided over ethnic issues, so Paul wrote to reset the foundation of how we are saved and how we live in light of God's grace. In the first two and a half chapters, Paul explains where we are without Christ.

It's a pretty dismal picture and honestly hard to read, but read we must. We must recognize our need for a Savior because no one is righteous and able to save themselves. But there is good news.

> *But now the righteousness of God has been manifested apart from the law, although the Law and the Prophets bear witness to it—the righteousness of God through faith in Jesus Christ for all who believe. For there is no distinction: for all have sinned and fall short of the glory of God, and are justified by his grace as a gift, through the redemption that is in Christ Jesus, whom God put forward as a propitiation by his blood, to be received by faith. This was to show God's righteousness, because in his divine forbearance he had passed over former sins. It was to show his righteousness at the present time, so that he might be just and the justifier of the one who has faith in Jesus.* Romans 3:21–26

"Through faith in Jesus Christ." There is no other way. We all fall short. We are all sinners. We all need a Savior. Praise God that He is faithful to save.

As we turn to Romans 4, Paul uses the example of Abraham to show that we need faith in order to be saved—that works will not save us. In making a covenant with Abraham (then called Abram), God said, "*Look toward heaven, and number the stars, if you are able to number them...So shall your offspring be*" (Genesis 15:5). Abraham responded in faith. "*And he believed the* LORD, *and he counted it to him as righteousness*" (Genesis 15:6). Paul points back to this moment when Abraham, the son of a pagan, confessed his faith in God.

> *No unbelief made him waver concerning the promise of God, but he grew strong in his faith as he gave glory to God, fully convinced that God was able to do what he had promised. That is why his faith was "counted to him as righteousness."*
> Romans 4:20–22

Many scholars consider this Abraham's moment of salvation—when he put his whole faith in God. No, he was not perfect in that moment. Yes, he continued to sin and make a lot of costly mistakes, but he trusted God and *grew* strong in his faith. This is a picture of what our faith looks like as we walk here on earth. It's a journey. From the time God called Abraham to the birth of Isaac spans twenty-four years.

Think back to where you were in your faith twenty-four years ago. How have you grown in faith?

The moment of salvation doesn't bring about perfection in our lives. Our faith will continue to grow as we continue to walk with God. God is faithful to save, but it starts with surrender and putting our faith in Him.

SOMETHING TO THINK ABOUT

Later in Romans, Paul explains what we must do to be saved:

If you confess with your mouth that Jesus is Lord and believe in your heart that God raised him from the dead, you will be saved. For with the heart one believes and is justified, and with the mouth one confesses and is saved.   Romans 10:9–10

We must confess with our mouths and believe in our hearts that Jesus died to pay the price of our sin, and that He was raised to life three days later. When we do this, we are saved. Then we spend the rest of our lives here on earth learning what it means to surrender and submit to our amazing God.

Don't discount the moment. Know that God is faithful to save, and then enjoy the rich benefits available to you, including the rest of the promises in this book. Each one of them is yours because you are saved by the grace of God through faith in Jesus Christ.

EXTRA VERSES FOR STUDY OR PRAYER

John 3:1–21; Ephesians 2:1–10

VERSE OF THE DAY

If you confess with your mouth that Jesus is Lord and believe in your heart that God raised him from the dead, you will be saved.   —Romans 10:9

PRAYER

This is a simple prayer of salvation. If you've never prayed this prayer or have more questions, you'll find a more detailed explanation in the appendix. If you have given your life to Jesus, I encourage you to read this as a prayer of rededication.

Jesus, thank You for coming and doing what I could not. You paid the price so that I might be saved, not just from hell, but for relationship with You. I believe in You, Lord Jesus. I confess that I am a sinner in desperate need of Your grace. Please save me. I give You my life and surrender to Your ways. Thank You for being faithful to save those who call on You.

THINK

_____

_____

_____

PRAY

_____

_____

_____

PRAISE

_____

_____

_____

TO-DO   PRAYER LIST

_____   _____

_____   _____

_____   _____

QUESTIONS FOR DEEPER REFLECTION

1. Do you struggle to believe that your faith is enough to save you? How does this promise reassure you that God is faithful to save you?

_____

_____

_____

2. When were you saved? How have you seen God grow your faith since that moment?

_____

_____

_____

DAY 2

GOD IS
FAITHFULLY PRESENT

And behold, I am with you always, to the end of the age.
—Matthew 28:20

I mentioned in the introduction that my family was facing yet another health crisis. This one concerned my youngest son, who was diagnosed with type 1 diabetes. It was more than a shock to us, and it completely uprooted our whole world. The first few months were filled with intense learning, pulling-my-hair-out frustration, and utter numbness. We were beyond exhausted, and I was struggling to keep it all together. In those days, I wasn't sitting down with God and having long, sweet times in the Word. Instead, I was leaning on the Word *in* me. I knew the importance of trusting the promises of God from our previous crisis. In those days when I could hardly think, the promise of God I kept coming back to was this one: God is faithful to be present. I knew God was with us, so my prayer was, "God, don't let me miss You. Let me see where You are."

In Matthew 28, before Jesus ascends into heaven, He gives His final charge to His disciples: go tell. Spread this good news. Take it to the nations. I think we often read this and feel the sense of purpose rise up in us. We feel emboldened and empowered, but I would imagine that those standing beside Jesus may have felt pure fear. They had been walking with Jesus for three years. He had been right there with them physically, and now He was leaving them. They were literally watching Him ascend *away* from them, but Jesus leaves them with this promise: *"I am with you always"* (Matthew 28:20).

He may have been leaving them physically, but He was not leaving them alone. He promised to be with them—and He promises us that too.

The story of the Bible is the story of the God who longs to dwell with His people and wants His people to dwell with Him. He *wants* to be with us, and through the life, death, and resurrection of Jesus Christ, He has made a way for us to do this. In her book, *Even Better Than Eden*, Nancy Guthrie further explains this truth:

> The great passion of God's heart, as revealed from Genesis to Revelation, is to be at home with his people in a place where nothing can separate or alienate or contaminate, enjoying a face-to-face relationship of pure joy with no goodbyes. In fact one of the most amazing things about the story we read in the Bible is that it is much more about God's desire to dwell with his people than about his people's desire to dwell with him.[2]

No goodbyes. No separation. With us. Always.[3]

I prayed to see God in my most desperate moments, and God graciously answered. I cannot explain the supernatural strength we seemed to have despite our physical and mental exhaustion. I could literally *feel* God holding us up. One of the early days on this journey, I had had enough. I was overwhelmed. My husband and I had just had a little *discussion*, and I needed a break. So I did what many of us women sometimes do in tense situations: I went shopping. In my head, I was debating what I would say if I ran into someone I knew. Would I tell the truth when they politely asked, "How are you?"

2. Nancy Guthrie, Even Better Than Eden: Nine Ways the Bible's Story Changes Everything about Your Story (Wheaton, IL: Crossway, 2018).
3. If you want to study this concept further, check out "To Dwell in Our Midst: A Study of the Tabernacle and How It Points Us to Jesus" at erinhwarren.com/dwell.

I turned a corner in the office supplies section, and there was an old friend from church. She was the kind of friend you couldn't hide the truth from. I started crying right there between the pens and craft supplies, telling her everything that had happened that week. She, in turn, gave me the exact encouragement from the Bible I needed that day. I could have lied to her. I could have chosen to walk away, believing it to be a coincidence. But God had answered my prayer. He reminded me that He was right there with me.

God's reminders can be the timely word of a friend, a text with a Bible verse you needed in that moment, or an unexplainable peace or strength that couldn't come from anyone else but God.

SOMETHING TO THINK ABOUT

God's promise in Matthew 28:20 is echoed in Hebrews 13:5: *"For he has said, 'I will never leave you nor forsake you.'"* When we face hardships and *feel* like God is absent, we can know beyond a shadow of a doubt that He has not left us or forsaken us. He is with us— always. Psalm 143:5 says, *"I remember the days of old; I meditate on all that you have done; I ponder the work of your hands."* When you are tempted to believe that God has broken this promise to you, go back to these verses and remember that God is faithfully present. Keep a list of all the ways you have seen Him with you, so that you can recall His faithfulness. Ask Him to open your eyes to see His tangible presence with you.

EXTRA VERSES FOR STUDY OR PRAYER

Psalm 23; Psalm 143:5–6; Hebrews 13:5–6

VERSE OF THE DAY

And behold, I am with you always, to the end of the age.
—Matthew 28:20

PRAYER

God, I know that You are faithful to be with me. Let me not miss You in the moments of my day. Help my eyes search for and see You. Help my ears listen to and hear You. Help my heart and mind to hold fast to the truth that You never leave or forsake me. Thank You for making the way for Your presence to be with us always, even to the end of the age.

THINK

_____

_____

_____

PRAY

_____

_____

_____

PRAISE

_____

_____

_____

TO-DO   PRAYER LIST

_____   _____

_____   _____

_____   _____

QUESTIONS FOR DEEPER REFLECTION

1. In what ways have you seen God's presence with you in your hard circumstances?

_____

_____

_____

2. When do you struggle to believe that God is with you? How can you use these verses to remind you of His faithful presence?

_____

_____

_____

DAY 3

GOD IS FAITHFUL
TO GIVE REST

*Come to me, all who labor and are heavy laden, and I will give
you rest. Take my yoke upon you, and learn from me, for I am
gentle and lowly in heart, and you will find rest for your souls.
For my yoke is easy, and my burden is light.*
—Matthew 11:28–30

If there has ever been a time when I've desperately felt the need for
rest, it is right now. Between writing, managing my family's health,
driving everywhere, running all the errands—and, oh, you want to
eat too?—I'm exhausted. But I've learned that our exhaustion is not
always a sign that we've said *yes* to too many things. Our natural inclination is to think we need to do less, but life with a special needs child
doesn't lend itself to physical rest. For me, in this season, physical
rest just isn't possible, but that doesn't mean God won't fulfill His
promise of rest.

These words of Jesus in Matthew 11 bring such a sigh of relief.
Another translation of verse 28 (NIV) invites those who are *"weary"*
to come to Jesus—meaning those who are tired, exhausted with toil,
burdens, and grief. *"Heavy laden"* literally means loaded up with
burdens. We are loaded up and burdened with illness, work, heavy
hearts, grief, rituals, and life itself. Notice that Jesus doesn't say He
will take away the burden. Instead, He promises us rest. Under His
yoke, we find the weight of the burden lifted. But what is this burden?

We usually stop reading at the end of Matthew 11, but if we turn to Matthew 12, we find that Jesus speaks these famous words in the context of the Sabbath. I think this is key to understanding the promised rest that Jesus is referencing here. Jewish law mandated a Sabbath every seven days as laid out in the Ten Commandments. (See Exodus 20:8–10.) Over the years, the Jewish religious leaders had added over three hundred laws to define what constituted work on the Sabbath. In addition, there were also sacrifices and cleansing rituals required in order for the people to keep pure. The burden of religion was heavy.

The yoke God's people were under—this yoke of the law, perfectionism, and living up to a certain standard—was not restful, but Jesus came to redefine Sabbath. He can do that because He is *"Lord of the Sabbath"* (Matthew 12:8 NIV). He came to free us from the ritualistic burden of religion and offer us His grace-filled relationship of rest. He came to release us from having to carry it all. He came to give us a new yoke—one that is easy and light. Our gentle and lowly Savior came to make a way so that God's presence would be with us always, without us having to work for it. We always have rest because we always have the presence of God with us. (See Exodus 33:14.)

SOMETHING TO THINK ABOUT

Sabbath is not binge-watching a show, doing an activity that relaxes you, or merely not working. True Sabbath rest is found when we allow the Creator of the world to breathe the breath of life over us. We do not have to carry it all alone. We do not have to earn our own salvation. We can come to Jesus, give Him our burdens, and learn how to walk in His ways. Jeremiah 6:16 says, *"Thus says the LORD: 'Stand by the roads, and look, and ask for the ancient paths, where the good way is; and walk in it, and find rest for your souls.'"*

Come to Jesus. Let Him breathe over you. Just as God breathed His breath into Adam and brought life, so His presence breathes life to give you rest. Sabbath is remembering who He is and what He has done for you. It's the covenant relationship you get to experience because of the blood of Jesus Christ. When you take time to cease and sit in His presence, you will find rest for your soul. Keep eternity in mind and rest, knowing who God is and His goals for you.

EXTRA VERSES FOR STUDY OR PRAYER

Exodus 31:12–17; Exodus 33:14; Jeremiah 6:16

VERSE OF THE DAY

Come to me, all who labor and are heavy laden, and I will give you rest. Take my yoke upon you, and learn from me, for I am gentle and lowly in heart, and you will find rest for your souls. For my yoke is easy, and my burden is light.

—Matthew 11:28–30

PRAYER

Lord, let Your presence be with me today. Breathe restful life over my soul. May I remember that I do not need to carry the burdens I feel; instead, I can lay them at Your feet, take Your yoke, and rest. Thank You for coming to redefine Sabbath rest. Thank You for showing us the way in which we should walk. Thank You for the promise of rest even when I feel anything but rested.

THINK

PRAY

PRAISE

_____

_____

_____

TO-DO

_____

_____

_____

PRAYER LIST

_____

_____

_____

QUESTIONS FOR DEEPER REFLECTION

1. How have you seen God's life-giving rest refresh you even when you are physically tired and weary?

_____

_____

2. In what areas of your life do you feel weary? How can you cease and lay those burdens down at His feet?

_____

_____

DAY 4

GOD IS FAITHFUL TO GO BEFORE YOU

*It is the LORD who goes before you. He will be with you; he will
not leave you or forsake you. Do not fear or be dismayed.*
—Deuteronomy 31:8

I had been teaching Bible study online solidly for almost two years when I felt a stirring from the Lord that I needed to take the summer off. For weeks, I told God that He was wrong. We were just hitting our stride. The ministry had momentum. Women were asking me what was next. They were eager to keep going. So taking a break made absolutely no sense! But God kept pushing. I heard it in a podcast, a sermon, and a social media post. *Take the summer off, Erin.* Finally, I couldn't ignore Him anymore, so I announced that I would be taking the summer off. I thought I would be using this time to focus on writing and resting, but two weeks after our last session, I was sitting in the doctor's office with my very sick, then seven-year-old son, who was diagnosed with type 1 diabetes. Instantly, I knew that God had gone before me when He said to take a break.

God's presence is with us, before and behind us. God is eternal, meaning He is timeless, or beyond time. When we talk about Him being omnipresent, it's not just that He's everywhere right now, but He's everywhere in time too. It's a big concept!

In Deuteronomy 31, Moses is giving his final speech to the Israelites and commissioning Joshua as their new leader. You can hear the urgency in his voice, the call to keep going, keep obeying, and keep their eyes on God. I imagine they were scared. While their numbers were great, they had been a nation without land. They had been wandering in the wilderness for forty years and were about to go to war. But Moses assured them that the Lord had gone before them.

God promised this land—and in Genesis 15:14, He promised judgment on those who were not following Him. Now, God was fulfilling His promises. He had already prepared the way. I love how Moses says, *"The LORD your God **himself** will go over before you"* (Deuteronomy 31:3). God wasn't sending an angel or a representative. God was leading the way, so they had nothing to fear. They would not be on this journey alone. They would not face their enemy alone. The weight of victory was not on their shoulders. God Himself was with them and before them. All they had to do was follow Him.

After we received my son's diabetes diagnosis, I didn't spend the summer writing and resting as I had planned. Our world was upended. There were so many times I thanked God for leading me to take a break. I was exhausted—mentally, physically, and emotionally. There was no way I could have taught Bible study *and* been present for my family in that season. But God knew. In Psalm 139, David praises God for His omniscience and omnipresence.

> *Even before a word is on my tongue, behold, O LORD, you know it altogether. You hem me in, behind and before, and lay your hand upon me.*   Psalm 139:4–5

I love the image of God hemming us in. It means there is no side of you that His presence does not cover. It means God is already there in every room you walk into and every situation you face. He knows every fear and every unknown ahead of you. He knows what words will be spoken.

His hand is upon you. You need not fear or be dismayed.

SOMETHING TO THINK ABOUT

During a recent conversation, my thirteen-year-old said, "You know how you didn't know something exists, then you learn about it, and suddenly, you start seeing it everywhere?" Oh, yes! And this phenomenon applies to this promise of God. When we know He goes before us, we will start to see His presence before us.

In our moments of crisis, it's easy to forget. That's why I keep a list of ways I have seen God go before me. I encourage you to do the same, whether in a journal or on your phone. You'll be amazed at the ways you see Him with you and before you. Because the Lord your God Himself goes before you, you can faithfully walk in obedience in what He calls you to do.

EXTRA VERSES FOR STUDY OR PRAYER

Psalm 139

VERSE OF THE DAY

It is the LORD who goes before you. He will be with you; he will not leave you or forsake you. Do not fear or be dismayed.
—Deuteronomy 31:8

PRAYER

Lord, I know You are faithful to go before me, so please open my eyes to see all the paths You have prepared for me. Please help me walk in confidence, not fear. Give me strength to walk in obedience to Your Word.

THINK

PRAY

_____

_____

_____

PRAISE

_____

_____

_____

TO-DO   PRAYER LIST

_____   _____

_____   _____

_____   _____

QUESTIONS FOR DEEPER REFLECTION

1. In your current situation, how have you seen God go before you?

_____

_____

_____

2. What step of obedience is He asking you to take? How can you step forward in faith knowing He's already there?

_____

_____

_____

DAY 5

GOD IS FAITHFUL
TO FORGIVE

*If we confess our sins, he is faithful and just and will forgive us
our sins and purify us from all unrighteousness.
If we claim we have not sinned, we make him out to be a liar
and his word is not in us.*
—1 John 1:9–10 (NIV)

My mind loves to remind me of all the times I fail, especially when my head hits the pillow at night. My world is finally still, and the silence gives way to a barrage of thoughts and memories. *Here's where you could have done better today. You messed up here. Should have said that then. Remember that time in eighth grade when you made fun of that kid? How can you think you can be a witness for Christ when in college you did THAT?!*

All I want is to sleep, but instead, my mind attacks. There is a promise I hold on to as darkness threatens to close in, a promise I throw in the face of my past sin.

God is faithful to forgive me.

The Greek word for *sin* literally means "to miss the mark." Y'all, I miss that mark daily...probably hourly. But what's so promising about today's Scripture from John is that he doesn't tell us we're liars if we *have* sinned. Instead, he says if we *say* we have *not* sinned, we are calling *God* a liar. It does us no good to think we do not sin. It does not benefit us to say we walk in light when we truly walk in darkness.

In fact, John tells us this *hinders* our fellowship with God and with one another. It threatens our joy.

God knows we are going to miss the mark. That's why He sent Jesus. It is only by His blood that we can be cleansed or purified from our sin. This is such a big promise because He not only promises forgiveness, He promises to purify us of the sin. The word *purify* means "to remove contaminants from." It's the idea of removing what is impure—the sin. His forgiveness means He no longer keeps our sin in our record. He disregards it.

God is the One who is faithful, just, and righteous. Only God, who is guiltless, is worthy and able to forgive. And He is faithful to do it.

SOMETHING TO THINK ABOUT

The catalyst for this forgiveness is our confession. In Psalm 32, David gives such a perfect picture of what happens when we do not confess our sins:

> *For when I kept silent, my bones wasted away through my groaning all day long. For day and night your hand was heavy upon me; my strength was dried up as by the heat of summer.*
> Psalm 32:3–4

Failing to confess our sins keeps us in the dark. Like my thoughts that come crawling out at night, sin steals our strength and makes us groan when we literally feel its weight upon us.

First John beckons us to step out of the darkness of our sin and step into the light of fellowship with the Father. *"But if we walk in the light, as he is in the light...the blood of Jesus, his Son, purifies us from all sin"* (1 John 1:7 NIV). It's even the inspiration for one of my favorite '90s songs by one of my favorite '90s bands.

> *I wanna be in the Light*
> *As You are in the Light*
> *I wanna shine like the stars in the heavens*

Oh, Lord be my light and be my salvation
'Cause all I want is to be in the Light[4]

We can trust God when we bring our sin to Him. It is the enemy who heaps shame and guilt on top of our sin, but our gracious God forgives us.

I acknowledged my sin to you, and I did not cover my iniquity;
I said, "I will confess my transgressions to the LORD," and you
forgave the iniquity of my sin.   Psalm 32:5

When we walk in His light, submit to His ways, and allow Him to teach us and guide us, we get to freely experience fellowship with our heavenly Father and with each other. In that, our joy is made complete. It's not fun to admit our faults, but the lifted weight is so worth it. Because God is Light and is faithful to forgive, we can step out of darkness and confess our sin to Him. *"Blessed is the one whose transgression is forgiven, whose sin is covered"* (Psalm 32:1).

EXTRA VERSES FOR STUDY OR PRAYER

Psalm 32

VERSE OF THE DAY

If we confess our sins, he is faithful and just and will forgive us
our sins and purify us from all unrighteousness. If we claim we
have not sinned, we make him out to be a liar and his word is not
in us.   —1 John 1:9–10 (NIV)

PRAYER

Father, thank You that I can come and confess my sin without fear. Your forgiveness is promised. Lord, I confess before You that I have missed the mark. Please forgive me. Help me walk in Your light. Teach me and guide me as I do. Let

---

4. DC Talk, "In the Light" on *Jesus Freak* (ForeFront/Virgin, 1995).

Your steadfast love surround me as I trust in You. I shout for joy that in Your forgiveness, I can experience fellowship with You.

THINK

_____

_____

_____

PRAY

_____

_____

_____

PRAISE

_____

_____

_____

TO-DO   PRAYER LIST

_____   _____

_____   _____

_____   _____

QUESTIONS FOR DEEPER REFLECTION

1. When have you seen God's faithful forgiveness lift the weight of sin and help you walk in His light?

---

2. What sin do you need to confess before your faithful Father?

DAY 6

GOD FAITHFULLY
GIVES US THE HOLY SPIRIT

And I will ask the Father, and he will give you another Helper,
to be with you forever, even the Spirit of truth, whom the world
cannot receive, because it neither sees him nor knows him. You
know him, for he dwells with you and will be in you.
—John 14:16–17

There have been many times when someone would give me a little pep talk and inevitably say, "God doesn't give you more than you can handle." Oh, how I wanted that to be true! I would be facing something difficult and hear this platitude meant to *encourage* me. It was as if they were saying that I had what it took to face a given situation because, otherwise, God wouldn't have allowed me to go through it. Sometimes, I was told, "God gives His hardest battles to His strongest soldiers."

Aside from the fact that this isn't true, the problem is that it only made me feel worse. If God thinks I can handle this, why am I struggling? Does God think I am a strong soldier when I am clearly falling apart over here? I don't know about you, but I cannot handle what life has thrown at me. Maybe you feel that too? Here's the truth: you cannot handle your life on your own.

This is the whole story of the Bible! When we read from Genesis to Revelation, we see people trying and failing time after time. It is only through Jesus that we are able to face what is coming.

As Jesus prepares to go to the cross, He spends one last evening pouring into His disciples. We find the story of the Last Supper in all four gospels, but only John devotes five whole chapters to the conversation they had that night. And there, in that upper room, when Jesus tells the disciples He is going away, He says something profound, scary, and unimaginable: this is for their good because God is going to send a Counselor to them, the Holy Spirit. In John 14:16, Jesus calls the Holy Spirit *"another Helper."* This comes from the Greek word *paraklétos,* meaning "to call to one's aid." It carries the idea of being "close beside." This Helper is not far off, not sitting in heaven and shouting down suggestions and good tidbits of advice. No, the Holy Spirit is not only near us—He is *in* us!

Peppered throughout this conversation, we see Jesus remind the disciples again and again that the Holy Spirit is coming to help them—and us. The Holy Spirit speaks truth, teaches us, and helps us remember what we've learned. The Holy Spirit guides us, convicts us, and reminds us who Jesus is. The Holy Spirit leads us to righteousness, judges, and declares the Word of God to us.

When life doesn't make sense, or when I have questions, or when I am at the end of myself, He is right there with me, giving me what I need to keep going, reminding me of the truth, guiding me as I traverse the wilderness, and convicting me of the areas in which I continue to trust myself instead of trusting Him.

SOMETHING TO THINK ABOUT

You do not have to face this life on your own because you're *not* alone! You have the Holy Spirit inside you. The Spirit who hovered over the chaos before the world was created, the Spirit who held back the waters of the Red Sea, the Spirit who raised Jesus from the dead, the Spirit who was in John as he wrote the words we've studied today—this same Spirit lives in you, me, your pastor, and everyone who declares Jesus as their Savior. He is there to help you face whatever lies ahead.

EXTRA VERSES FOR STUDY OR PRAYER

John 15:18–27; John 16:7–15

VERSE OF THE DAY

And I will ask the Father, and he will give you another Helper, to be with you forever, even the Spirit of truth, whom the world cannot receive, because it neither sees him nor knows him. You know him, for he dwells with you and will be in you.

—John 14:16–17

PRAYER

Holy Spirit, thank You for Your presence alongside me. I cannot handle what is before me, but I know You can. Please teach me and guide me through Your Word. Please let me hear the truth and not be swayed by the lies of the world. Give me strength to move forward, even when I cannot see the way. Show me the sin that entangles my feet so that I can shake off my flesh and rely more on You.

THINK

PRAY

PRAISE

_____
_____
_____

TO-DO

_____
_____
_____

PRAYER LIST

_____
_____
_____

QUESTIONS FOR DEEPER REFLECTION

1. In what ways have you seen the Holy Spirit carry you, guide you, teach you, or speak truth in a situation that felt overwhelming?

_____
_____
_____

2. Which of these roles of the Holy Spirit brings comfort to you in your current situation?

_____
_____
_____

DAY 7

GOD FAITHFULLY GIVES PEACE

*Do not be anxious about anything, but in everything by prayer
and supplication with thanksgiving let your requests be made
known to God. And the peace of God,
which surpasses all understanding, will guard your hearts
and your minds in Christ Jesus.*
—Philippians 4:6–7

I have a tendency to make mountains out of molehills. When I am confronted with hardship, my mind immediately wants to go through every possible scenario. *What if this? What if that?* And my peace is gone. One of my mentors, Rosalie, once told me, "Don't let the 'what if' horse out of the barn. It's hard to reign it back in." She is right. It's hard to hold onto peace when our mind is racing within us.

I think peace is one of those words that seems arbitrary or hard to define. We think of it as tranquility or getting along; we declare, "All I want is world peace!" But the peace spoken of in Scripture is so much more than that.

There are countless Scriptures in the Bible about peace. I think our go-to verses when we face hardship or a wilderness season are in Philippians 4. We say, "Pray about it. Give it to God, and then you will get the peace that passes understanding." But I think we often still don't *feel* at peace. Peace is a promise, so peace *is* possible no matter the storm we are facing. Peace is possible *in the midst of* chaos and hardship and exhaustion. So how do we experience the peace that Paul is talking about in the Scripture for today? We must turn our minds from our problems and instead think on the things of God.

> *Finally, brothers, whatever is true, whatever is honorable, whatever is just, whatever is pure, whatever is lovely, whatever is commendable, if there is any excellence, if there is anything worthy of praise, think about these things. What you have learned and received and heard and seen in me—practice these things, and the God of peace will be with you.*   Philippians 4:8–9

Our mind is a battlefield, and Satan relishes the chance to wage war in our thoughts, to continually tempt us to think that what we have is not enough, our situation is too dire, or peace is a lie. Let's not forget: the God of peace is with us. His peace already lives inside us. We must shift our thinking and steadfastly keep our minds focused on our trustworthy God.

> *You will keep in perfect peace those whose minds are steadfast, because they trust in you. Trust in the LORD forever, for the LORD, the LORD himself, is the Rock eternal.*   Isaiah 26:3–4 NIV

This is my *sword of truth* verse, which I use to refocus my mind when my thoughts start to stray. There's something that we miss in the English translation of this verse: *"perfect peace"* in Hebrew is *shalom shalom*. This repeated use of the word adds emphasis and signifies the completeness of the topic. The Hebrew concept of peace is much more than a tranquil state. *Shalom* is best described in English as "completeness, soundness." It's whole or undivided. So the repeated use of *shalom* here signifies that our trust or faith in God allows us to be completely whole, completely undivided. We experience peace when our mind is wholly focused on God, not our circumstances, and we steadfastly keep it there. We must firmly root our faith and our focus on our God of Peace.

SOMETHING TO THINK ABOUT

Is peace truly possible in the chaos of life and motherhood? The answer is yes. As my friend Brooke McGlothlin so poignantly points out in her book, *Everyday Prayers for Peace*,[5] "Jesus Himself *is* our peace."

> *Therefore, since we have been justified by faith, we have peace with God through our Lord Jesus Christ.*   Romans 5:1

Before we can experience the peace *of* God, we must first have peace *with* God. We were sinners, separated from God, but through Jesus and our profession of faith in Him, we are no longer at war with God. We are no longer His enemy. We are brought near, and Jesus is our peace. Because of that, we can also experience the peace *of* God.

As Jesus is preparing His disciples for His arrest and crucifixion, He tells them:

> *Peace I leave with you; my peace I give to you. Not as the world gives do I give to you. Let not your hearts be troubled, neither let them be afraid.*   John 14:27

The peace we experience is rooted in the finishing work of the cross. We need not be troubled. We need not fear. We need not have divided hearts and minds. We do not have to worry about what is to come, whether storms or judgment. We are completely whole because we have Jesus. Because God faithfully made us whole again, we can be completely at peace.

EXTRA VERSES FOR STUDY OR PRAYER

Isaiah 26; John 14:7; Romans 5:1

VERSE OF THE DAY

> *Do not be anxious about anything, but in everything by prayer and supplication with thanksgiving let your requests be made known*

---

5. Brooke McGlothlin, *Everyday Prayers for Peace* (New Kensington, PA: Whitaker House, 2022).

to God. And the peace of God, which surpasses all understanding, will guard your hearts and your minds in Christ Jesus.
—Philippians 4:6–7

PRAYER

Jesus, thank You for being our peace. Without You, peace is not possible, but because of Your Holy Spirit in me, I know I can have complete peace, no matter what I am facing. Please help me think on things that are true, honorable, just, pure, lovely, commendable, excellent, and praiseworthy. Help me remain steadfastly, wholly, and firmly fixed on You, my trustworthy Rock eternal.

THINK

PRAY

PRAISE

TO-DO

PRAYER LIST

QUESTIONS FOR DEEPER REFLECTION

1. Where do you feel your heart and mind divided and not at peace?

----

2. When have you experienced God's unexplainable peace in the face of hard circumstances in the past? How does that help you remain steadfast in your trust and faith in the God of peace now?

DAY 8

GOD IS FAITHFUL IN SUFFERING

I have said these things to you, that in me you may have peace.
In the world you will have tribulation. But take heart;
I have overcome the world.
—John 16:33

I don't know where we got the notion that saying *yes* to God meant ease, comfort, a good life, and maybe even a little bit of wealth. Often when hardship comes along, we see it as punishment. When a faithful Sunday school teacher gets cancer, or a powerful missionary dies, or a Spirit-filled worship leader faces a health crisis, we say, "Why would God allow them to die? Why would God allow them to go through this? They did so much good for God." But the idea that our faith insulates us from all harm is not found in Scripture. Rather, the Bible is full of stories of people who faced hardship: famine, imprisonment, accusations, wilderness, barrenness, betrayal, health issues, and persecution, to name a few. There is not one story in the Bible where someone says, "God, I will follow you," and everything goes smoothly for the rest of their life.

As I began to read the Bible looking for God's promises, I was slightly shocked to learn that instead of a good life, we are promised suffering, tribulation, and hard times.

John 16:33 was my friend Lynda's life verse. She always proudly claimed it and used it frequently to encourage her friends. To her,

Jesus's words weren't mere platitudes to make us feel better when things weren't going our way; they expressed a deep conviction. God had proven His faithfulness during times of hardship over and over throughout her life. She passed away on September 12, 2021, and this verse is her legacy. I can still see the confidence well up inside her as she prepared to quote this verse to yet another suffering friend. And she always ended with, "Did you know that is my life verse?" And we would chuckle because everyone knew.

I think the context of this verse, though, is what gives weight to the hope it reveals. These are Jesus's last recorded words to the disciples before He prays to the Father, anticipating what lies ahead. John 13–17 contains what is known as the Upper Room Discourse. Jesus has washed His disciples' feet, predicted Judas's betrayal and Peter's denial, and shared the Passover meal, and now He begins telling them something frightening: He is going away. We went through this scene together on Day 6 as we learned about the promise of the Holy Spirit, but I want to focus on something a little different here.

I often think about the distress the disciples must have felt, how hard it must have been to learn that everything you thought was going to happen was wrong. But I recently heard a pastor teaching through this passage who pointed to a truth I had never considered: Jesus's distress. As Jesus says these words to His closest eleven friends, He knows their future. Jesus, being God, is omniscient, which means He is all-knowing. Jesus knows that ten of those men are going to die horrific deaths because of their faith in Him. They are going to be martyrs. Jesus is looking into the eyes of men who are going to change the world, yes, but because of this, they are going to pay the highest cost. He knows John will live out his days in exile on the island of Patmos. He knows their lives are going to be marked by suffering. So, He leaves them with hope.

SOMETHING TO THINK ABOUT

Jesus tells the disciples what is going to happen so that, when it does, they won't be tempted to fall away. Jesus assures them they will not be left as orphans but will have the Holy Spirit to guide them. He says, *"You will be sorrowful, but your sorrow will turn into joy"* (John 16:20). He says these things so they can have peace. Peace means peace of mind, quietness, and rest, but for the Jewish people, it also carries the idea of completeness. Peace is possible even in the midst of the storm because Jesus overcame the world. He is victorious.

So, take heart, sister. Move forward in courage. Do not be surprised by the trouble, the trial, the tribulation, or the suffering. Do not sink into despair. He is faithful even in suffering. Because Jesus has overcome, you can have peace.

EXTRA VERSES FOR STUDY OR PRAYER

Second Corinthians 12:6–10

VERSE OF THE DAY

I have said these things to you, that in me you may have peace. In the world you will have tribulation. But take heart; I have overcome the world. —John 16:33

PRAYER

Jesus, thank You for the peace that is available to us, even in our suffering. I know I will face hardship in this world. Let me not despair or question Your faithfulness. Let me remember that though this world brings trouble, I can have peace and courage because You have overcome the world. You are the victorious One!

THINK

PRAY

_____

_____

_____

PRAISE

_____

_____

_____

TO-DO   PRAYER LIST

_____   _____

_____   _____

_____   _____

QUESTIONS FOR DEEPER REFLECTION

1. Think of a time you went through a hardship. How does knowing Jesus overcame help you have the peace and courage to move forward?

_____

_____

_____

2. In what instances has suffering led you closer to God?

_____

_____

_____

DAY 9

GOD IS FAITHFUL
TO USE OUR SUFFERING

Not only that, but we rejoice in our sufferings, knowing that
suffering produces endurance, and endurance produces
character, and character produces hope, and hope does not put
us to shame, because God's love has been poured into our hearts
through the Holy Spirit who has been given to us.
—Romans 5:3–5

I've always had a bent toward the positive. In fact, it's one of my strengths. I can almost always find a silver lining, a good explanation, or a way to escape feeling any pain or hardship. I was really good at it until my husband Kris got sick. There's no escaping chronic illness. It was the first time I had to sit in my pain, and I hated it.

I wanted to know why. Why was God allowing this? Why did He think this was a good idea? I knew *"that for those who love God all things work together for good"* (Romans 8:28). Yada yada. *(Eye roll.)* But I was tired, stressed, carrying the weight of my family…and did I mention *tired*? I wanted to get to the point, learn the lesson, and get back to my happy, comfortable life. But I was stuck.

Then my friend Stacey sent me today's Scripture reading.

I had no feelings of joy about my present circumstances, and I couldn't imagine actually rejoicing that we were going through this. I wanted to know *why*, but God taught me to ask a different question: *How?* How are You using this? This theme that suffering has a purpose in our life is found in many places in Scripture. Here, Paul points us to the fact that suffering produces the ability to endure, to be steadfast and patient. God uses our suffering to help us grow firmly in our faith. We often think hardship makes our faith waver, but in fact, it makes it stronger.

James shares a similar truth:

> *Count it all joy, my brothers, when you meet trials of various kinds, for you know that the testing of your faith produces steadfastness. And let steadfastness have its full effect, that you may be perfect and complete, lacking in nothing.*　　James 1:2–4

The Greek word for *steadfast* means "to remain under." All those years I escaped the pain didn't help me grow endurance and steadfastness in my faith. I didn't "*let steadfastness have its full effect,*" and as a result, my faith was lacking. When the bigger storm came, I began to crumble; this time, I couldn't get out from under it. God used that time to shore up my faith, to deepen my roots in Him so I could be more patient, enduring through the subsequent trials that have come our way.

SOMETHING TO THINK ABOUT

When we grow in endurance, we also grow in character. Peter affirms this:

> *In this you rejoice, though now for a little while, if necessary, you have been grieved by various trials, so that the tested genuineness of your faith—more precious than gold that perishes though it is tested by fire—may be found to result in praise and glory and honor at the revelation of Jesus Christ.*　　—1 Peter 1:6–7

Trials have a way of refining us by removing impurities from our lives. Oh, I could write a whole book on this process! We have to let our hardships help us recognize our idols—the things we turn to instead of God for comfort, control, or confirmation. We have to partner with God in these trials and let the fire of difficulty point us back to the One who is everything we need. That's where we find hope. Our faith, our confidence in God, grows when we remain steadfast under trials and allow God to refine our character through them. The result will be a faith, a trust, and a hope that will not fail.

We may never know the answer to *why*, but we can trust that God will faithfully use the suffering in our lives for our good. The result will be a more solid and stable trust that God is who He says He is and does what He says He will do.

EXTRA VERSES FOR STUDY OR PRAYER

Romans 8:28; James 1:2–4; 1 Peter 1:3–9

VERSE OF THE DAY

Not only that, but we rejoice in our sufferings, knowing that suffering produces endurance, and endurance produces character, and character produces hope, and hope does not put us to shame, because God's love has been poured into our hearts through the Holy Spirit who has been given to us. —Romans 5:3–5

PRAYER

Lord, this world brings hurt and hardship and suffering, but You are the God who faithfully uses these fiery trials for our good. Let me see how You are using this even when I do not understand why. Build endurance and steadfastness in me. Reveal to me the places I need to cast off idols so I can be refined. Most of all, I put my full faith, my complete confidence, and my whole hope in You. Thank You for not failing me.

THINK

PRAY

PRAISE

TO-DO   PRAYER LIST

QUESTIONS FOR DEEPER REFLECTION

1. How have you seen God produce endurance, proven character, and hope in your life through trials?

---

2. What trial are you going through now? How can you release your desire for knowing why and instead seek how God is using it?

DAY 10

GOD FAITHFULLY CARES FOR YOU

The Lord is my shepherd; I shall not want. He makes me lie down in green pastures. He leads me beside still waters. He restores my soul. He leads me in paths of righteousness for his name's sake.
—Psalm 23:1–3

Anxiety is on the rise. That's probably not news to you. It feels like statistics are flying at us every day, showing increases across so many age categories—from kids to teens to young adults. I can feel the rise in me too. There are days when I have a pit in my stomach that I cannot explain. I feel on edge, unsure, nervous, and worried. Some days there are real issues facing me, but on other days, I cannot pinpoint the source of my unease.

But this is not how God wants us to live. He did not intend for us to carry these burdens. Peter tells us, *"Cast all your anxiety on him because he cares for you"* (1 Peter 5:7 NIV). The Greek word for *care* is related to concern. It implies attention or an inclination toward us.

God sees you, takes an interest in you, leans toward you, and desires to help you.

The description of an ancient shepherd in Psalm 23 offers one of the most incredible pictures of this concern and care in Scripture. David, who was a shepherd, gives us a picture of the beautiful ways our Shepherd cares for us.

Sheep require a shepherd for *everything*. They cannot find green pastures or water on their own. Likewise, we are helpless without our caring Shepherd, who provides everything we need. While this does include physical needs, He also provides for our spiritual needs. Everything we need for life is found in our Good Shepherd. Green pastures imply safety, refreshment, and sustenance. Still waters refer to waters of rest.

With God, your soul can be at rest. Even when you walk through dark valleys, He is with you. His care doesn't stop when you go through hard times. He still cares for you, guides you, and keeps the enemy at bay.

SOMETHING TO THINK ABOUT

Notice that in each of these examples from Psalm 23:1–3, it is God taking the action. We are not guiding or leading ourselves. We are not in charge of our own restoration. Our faithful, caring Shepherd is the One who provides. Our Good Shepherd is the One who leads and guides. He is the One who restores, the One whose presence provides peace and comfort. He is the source of it all. We, like sheep, cannot find it on our own.

But there's a caveat. Our Good Shepherd is not a cosmic genie, handing out good things to those who rub some magic lamp just right. The sheep must submit to His authority. The metaphor in Scripture is also one of lordship, not just care. Jesus is our Shepherd *and* our King. To all of us who listen to Him and follow Him, Jesus is *"the good shepherd* [who] *lays down his life for the sheep"* (John 10:11).

When you are tempted to believe God has forgotten you, or that He does not care what happens to you, or that He is not concerned about your life, remember your Good Shepherd. Listen to His voice. Remember the promise of His care and concern for you. You can follow Him, knowing that all you need is found in your faithful, caring Shepherd. Like David, you will hold fast to this truth:

> *Only goodness and faithful love will pursue me all the days of my life, and I will dwell in the house of the* Lord *as long as I live.*
> Psalm 23:6 csb

EXTRA VERSES FOR STUDY OR PRAYER
Ezekiel 34:30–31; John 10:1–18; 1 Peter 5:7

VERSE OF THE DAY

The LORD is my shepherd; I shall not want. He makes me lie down in green pastures. He leads me beside still waters. He restores my soul. He leads me in paths of righteousness for his name's sake. —Psalm 23:1–3

PRAYER

Lord, You are the Good Shepherd. I know that in You, I find all that I need. Even when I walk through hard times, You are with me. Thank You for Your faithful care over my life. When I find myself questioning You in fear, help me remember You are by my side, guiding me, providing for me, and restoring me. Help me hear Your voice and follow in submission as You lead me on the paths of righteousness. May it all bring glory to Your great name.

THINK

PRAY

PRAISE

_____

_____

_____

TO-DO   PRAYER LIST

_____   _____

_____   _____

_____   _____

QUESTIONS FOR DEEPER REFLECTION

1. How have you seen God faithfully care for you during a hard season in your life?

_____

_____

_____

2. In what areas of your life do you struggle to submit to the leadership of your Shepherd and King?

_____

_____

_____

DAY 11

GOD FAITHFULLY KEEPS YOU

*My sheep hear my voice, and I know them, and they follow me.
I give them eternal life, and they will never perish, and no one
will snatch them out of my hand. My Father, who has given
them to me, is greater than all, and no one is able to snatch
them out of the Father's hand.*
—John 10:27–29

One of my children is a keeper who never throws anything out. This child saves *everything*—all the toys, every stuffed animal, all the artwork, little pieces of paper with doodles on them, even tags from clothing. When it's time to clean said child's room, the task is often met with tears over losing these *treasures*. To this child, everything is precious.

Similarly, God is a keeper, and He faithfully keeps those who are in Him. You are precious to God.

Yesterday, we saw God as our Shepherd and our King, but one aspect of our Shepherd that we didn't address is that He does not lose one of His sheep. He promises us this in today's Scripture reading.

The enemy wants you to believe there is still separation between you and God. He comes like a thief, seeking to steal, kill, and destroy. (See John 10:10.) He wants to lure you away from your Good Shepherd, but he cannot do so. Satan will lie to you, saying that your sin is too great; he will try to make you believe God will cast you out.

He will try to kill your passion for God, steal your joy in all circumstances, and destroy your hope, but remember this: Your God is a keeper, and He faithfully keeps you.

> *Who shall separate us from the love of Christ? Shall tribulation, or distress, or persecution, or famine, or nakedness, or danger, or sword?...No, in all these things we are more than conquerors through him who loved us. For I am sure that neither death nor life, nor angels nor rulers, nor things present nor things to come, nor powers, nor height nor depth, nor anything else in all creation, will be able to separate us from the love of God in Christ Jesus our Lord.* Romans 8:35, 37–39

Nothing. Absolutely nothing can separate you from the God who faithfully keeps you. No matter what you are facing—whether hardship, persecution, lack, or danger—you are not separated from your Good Shepherd. You cannot be snatched from His hand, not now or in the future. There is nothing high, nothing low, or nothing created that can separate you from the God who keeps you.

SOMETHING TO THINK ABOUT

Remember the truth about sheep? They are prone to straying. They cannot find what they need on their own. As God's sheep, we are called to follow and submit. Jude gives us this charge:

> *But you, beloved, building yourselves up in your most holy faith and praying in the Holy Spirit, **keep yourselves in the love of God**, waiting for the mercy of our Lord Jesus Christ that leads to eternal life.* Jude 1:20–21

Keep yourself in the love of God. Do not stray from your Shepherd and your King. I know this world brings heartache and doubt. Most days, I long for Him to come back and finish what He started, but as we wait, let's not neglect our faith. Let's continue to grow in our faith and trust in our Savior, knowing we are kept in Him. The day of the Lord will come. With patience, let's wait on the

Lord, for nothing will separate us from Him, and no one can snatch us from His hand. Because God faithfully keeps us, we can keep ourselves in His faithful love.

EXTRA VERSES FOR STUDY OR PRAYER

John 6:36–40; Romans 8:35–39; Jude 1:20–21

VERSE OF THE DAY

My sheep hear my voice, and I know them, and they follow me. I give them eternal life, and they will never perish, and no one will snatch them out of my hand. My Father, who has given them to me, is greater than all, and no one is able to snatch them out of the Father's hand.   —John 10:27–29

PRAYER

Good Shepherd, You are a keeper, and in You, I am kept. No matter what I face today, it will not separate me from You. You play for keeps, and I am safe in Your hands. Help me continue building my most holy faith in You, praying daily, keeping in Your steadfast love as I patiently wait for the day You come for us.

THINK

_____

_____

_____

PRAY

_____

_____

_____

PRAISE

_____

_____

_____

TO-DO

_____

_____

_____

PRAYER LIST

_____

_____

_____

QUESTIONS FOR DEEPER REFLECTION

1. In what circumstances do you struggle to believe you are kept in Christ?

_____

_____

_____

2. How have you seen the enemy try to steal, kill, and destroy? What comfort does it bring to know that you cannot be snatched from the hand of your Good Shepherd?

_____

_____

_____

DAY 12

GOD IS FAITHFUL TO GIVE MERCY

But this I call to mind, and therefore I have hope:
the steadfast love of the Lord never ceases; his mercies never
come to an end; they are new every morning; great is your
faithfulness. "The Lord is my portion," says my soul, "therefore
I will hope in him."
—Lamentations 3:21–24

I am a wannabe plant lady. I love the idea of planting flowers and growing beautiful, green things. Sometimes this desire grows particularly strong, and I will find myself perusing the garden center at my local hardware store. My friend Natalie, who is a true plant lady, tipped me off to the clearance section, where nearly dead plants line racks with one last hope of being rescued. One day, clearly feeling confident in my abilities to be the one to give a plant new life, I picked up a flowering bush for a mere dollar. I brought it home and gave it a spot in the flower bed right next to my driveway.

Through no effort on my part, the nearly dead bush not only came back to life, but it began to flourish once out of the pot and rooted in soil, where it enjoyed sunshine and plenty of water provided by Florida's summer rains. Soon, it began to flower. This particular bush had both purple and white flowers, but even more interesting to me was the fact that every morning, it bloomed, and every evening, the flowers fell off. The next morning, as I backed my car out of the driveway, I would be greeted by new purple and white flowers. I honestly don't know this plant's real name, but I called it my *New Morning Mercies*. Every day, as I left the house, I was reminded that God's mercies are there waiting for me: purple for royalty, white for purity.

Lamentations is a book of lament. Written specifically to lament the fall of Judah to the Babylonians, the themes of lament translate to the dire situations of our lives today. Reading the third chapter, we can sense the depth of the pain:

> *I am the man who has seen affliction under the rod of his wrath; he has driven and brought me into darkness without any light; surely against me he turns his hand again and again the whole day long. He has made my flesh and my skin waste away; he has broken my bones; he has besieged and enveloped me with bitterness and tribulation; he has made me dwell in darkness like the dead of long ago.*   Lamentations 3:1–6

Under wrath. In darkness. Wasting away. Broken. Attacked. Surrounded. The situation seems grim. And yet, in the center of this book of mourning and crying out, in today's Scripture reading, we find the Light.

God's love never ceases, and His mercy never comes to an end. They are new every morning. He is faithful. Every morning when we wake up, His mercy is there waiting for us like my purple and white blooms. But unlike my flowers that faded every evening, His mercy is always there because He is merciful. We cannot use up or run out of His mercy. *"Every morning he shows forth his justice; each dawn he does not fail"* (Zephaniah 3:5).

SOMETHING TO THINK ABOUT

I have often wondered why the author of Lamentations says God's mercy never runs out if it is new every morning. Doesn't that imply that we use up His mercy throughout the day, and then it recharges overnight? Yet I think he uses this metaphor because when you wake up, before you've even sinned, before you even need it, His mercy is there waiting. You are already and always under His mercy.

We often define *mercy* as "not getting what we deserve." The big word for this is *forbearance*. His mercy is great, but we should recognize our need for mercy. We deserve to be under wrath, in darkness, wasting away, and broken. But Jesus. He stepped in and interceded on our behalf. He knew we were without hope, and in His unceasing, steadfast, faithful love, He came here, bearing with our sin, so that we would experience His mercy. Because God is faithfully merciful, I have hope.

EXTRA VERSES FOR STUDY OR PRAYER

Exodus 34:1–9; Zephaniah 3:5

VERSE OF THE DAY

But this I call to mind, and therefore I have hope: the steadfast love of the LORD *never ceases; his mercies never come to an end; they are new every morning; great is your faithfulness. "The* LORD *is my portion," says my soul, "therefore I will hope in him."*   —Lamentations 3:21–24

PRAYER

Lord, I do not deserve Your mercy, yet every morning, it is there waiting for me. You are faithful to be merciful because You *are* mercy. May I call this to mind every morning and cling to the hope I have in You. Thank You for Your great faithfulness that never comes to an end.

THINK

PRAY

_____

_____

_____

PRAISE

_____

_____

_____

TO-DO

_____

_____

_____

PRAYER LIST

_____

_____

QUESTIONS FOR DEEPER REFLECTION

1. How has God's faithful mercy given you hope?

_____

_____

_____

2. The Scripture reading for today has been a great comfort to me when I am walking through darkness. Write the names of a few friends who are facing hardships and pray these verses over them.

_____

_____

_____

DAY 13

GOD FAITHFULLY COMFORTS US

Blessed be the God and Father of our Lord Jesus Christ,
the Father of mercies and God of all comfort, who comforts us
in all our affliction, so that we may be able to comfort those who
are in any affliction, with the comfort with which
we ourselves are comforted by God.
—2 Corinthians 1:3–4

Hygge (pronounced *hyoo-gah*) is a Danish word that means comfort and coziness. It encompasses the idea of softness, contentment, and well-being. Denmark is known for its long, dark, and harsh winters, and *hygge* brings a sense of warmth and comfort when the outside circumstances are anything but. The key element to living a *hygge* lifestyle is the comfort that togetherness brings, gathering with others and sharing together even in the frigid winter.

While *hygge* is not a biblical concept, it does somewhat reflect biblical comfort. In the opening verses of his second letter to the church in Corinth, Paul calls God the *"God of all comfort."* In fact, he uses the word *comfort* ten times in the first six verses after his greeting. The church was facing great suffering and questioned God because of it. They were wrestling with the concept of suffering despite their faith in a God they believed was good. So, when Paul began his letter, he recognized their despair and the darkness they faced and pointed them to God as their Comforter.

But what is the comfort God gives us? When we think of comfort, we think of something easing our burden or making us feel better in the face of grief or hard circumstances. In fact, the Greek word used here is *paraklésis,* a derivative of the same word used to describe the Holy Spirit as our Helper. If you recall, it means "to call to one's aid," and comes from two root words that literally mean "close beside." His comfort is His presence. He is *"near to the brokenhearted and saves the crushed in spirit"* (Psalm 34:18) and blesses *"those who mourn, for they shall be comforted"* (Matthew 5:4).

We've established that suffering is part of life here on earth. We will be faced with trials and tribulations and hardships. But as much as we share in suffering, we also share in God's comfort. And this is not just any comfort. His comfort is abundant!

For as we share abundantly in Christ's sufferings, so through Christ we share abundantly in comfort too. 2 Corinthians 1:5

The comfort God gives is over and above what we need. His presence provides an abundance of comfort for us. In my own life, I have seen His presence bring comfort countless times, and when people ask me to pray over certain situations, my prayer always includes, "Let them see Your tangible presence." *That* is what brings contentment and well-being when we are facing a harsh season. *That* is what allows our hope to be unshaken; suffering is promised, but so is His comfort. (See 2 Corinthians 1:7.)

SOMETHING TO THINK ABOUT

There's an aspect of *hygge* comfort that happens in community, and the same goes for comfort in the church. Part of God's plan for our comfort during the harsh seasons of life is that we, as the body of Christ, would come together and comfort one another. Paul says we have been comforted, *"so that we may be able to comfort those who are in any affliction, with the comfort with which we ourselves are comforted by God"* (2 Corinthians 1:4).

Because His comfort is abundant, we can also comfort one another, knowing the comfort won't run out. We need to walk close beside one another. As my family and I have continued to walk through crises, the greatest gift has been the people who enter into the hardships with us. They sit with us in our suffering, not offering platitudes or silver linings, but simply saying, "I'm sorry you are going through this. This is hard."

EXTRA VERSES FOR STUDY OR PRAYER

Psalm 34; Matthew 5:4; 2 Thessalonians 2:16–17

VERSE OF THE DAY

Blessed be the God and Father of our Lord Jesus Christ, the Father of mercies and God of all comfort, who comforts us in all our affliction, so that we may be able to comfort those who are in any affliction, with the comfort with which we ourselves are comforted by God. —2 Corinthians 1:3–4

PRAYER

God of comfort, thank You for Your presence with me in my suffering. You come to my aid and remain close beside me. You are not far, and Your salvation is here. As I grieve and face hardship, may I remember that Your presence with me is an abundant comfort, lifting the weight of the burden, giving me strength and joy. Give me eyes to see my brothers and sisters in their suffering as well and strength to sit with them as an extension of Your comfort.

THINK

PRAY

PRAISE

TO-DO   ## PRAYER LIST

------------------------   ------------------------
------------------------   ------------------------
------------------------   ------------------------

QUESTIONS FOR DEEPER REFLECTION

1. Who has been a comfort to you as you walk through a
   harsh season?

----

2. Pray and ask the Lord to show you who needs His comfort. Write their names here and reach out to be His presence with them.

DAY 14

GOD IS FAITHFULLY VICTORIOUS

No, in all these things we are more than conquerors
through him who loved us.
—Romans 8:37

was not super athletic growing up; being good at sports was not my gifting. Because I'm tall, people often ask me if I played volleyball or basketball in high school, and my response is always an emphatic, chuckling, "No!" With my lanky, uncoordinated arms and legs, I was always in the last bunch to be picked. I pretty much knew anytime I played a sport, I was going to lose. Defeat was inevitable. Thank goodness the same is not true in our faith. In Romans 8:31–39, Paul tells us that, as Christians, we are victorious!

> *What then shall we say to these things? If God is for us, who can be against us? He who did not spare his own Son but gave him up for us all, how will he not also with him graciously give us all things? Who shall bring any charge against God's elect? It is God who justifies. Who is to condemn? Christ Jesus is the one who died—more than that, who was raised—who is at the right hand of God, who indeed is interceding for us…No, in all these things we are more than conquerors through him who loved us.* Romans 8:31–34, 37

More than conquerors. This isn't a nail-biter. This isn't a close game. Jesus is not throwing up a hero shot for a buzzer-beating win.

The Greek word here is derived from two root words: *hyper*, meaning "abundance," and *nikao*, meaning "victory." Jesus has won the abundant, overwhelming victory. This is no contest; this is a blowout.

The pain point here is that we are living in the in-between. The victory has been won, but we aren't living in eternity yet. This world is still broken and full of pain; it may seem like Satan is winning. Your life may not *feel* victorious, but His victory is sure. We know that Jesus is *sitting* at the right hand of the Father. (See Mark 16:19.) This is an indication that the work is done, and the victory is won—not just for a little while, not just until next year's championship game, but for all eternity.

Because God is for us and Christ interceded on our behalf, we have the overwhelming victory too. By our faith in Him and His victory, we overcome.

> *For everyone who has been born of God overcomes the world. And this is the victory that has overcome the world—our faith. Who is it that overcomes the world except the one who believes that Jesus is the Son of God?* 1 John 5:4–5

Death doesn't have the final word anymore. Sin doesn't have the final word. Persecution doesn't have the final word. Distress doesn't have the final word. Sickness doesn't have the final word. Nothing and no one will take away Jesus's victory. Jesus took our punishment. Jesus took our shame. Jesus was the one who was condemned in our place, and when He walked out of the grave, His victory and ours was sealed forever. We can overcome the world by faith in our victorious God.

SOMETHING TO THINK ABOUT

While I am not good at sports, I do enjoy watching them. You can always tell which team lost by the way the players walk off the court or the field. Their heads are down, shoulders slumped. When the stakes are high, there are often tears, and losing players hide their faces under towels. But the winning team almost jumps off the court or field with heads held high. They leap in the air, arms flailing in victory, high-fiving one another, and pumping up the crowd. There's a difference between the posture of defeat and the posture of victory. We do not have to walk around feeling downcast and defeated. We get to walk around cheering with our heads held high because God wins. All the praise hands! We are more than conquerors. Because God has the surpassing victory, we can walk in a posture of victory too.

EXTRA VERSES FOR STUDY OR PRAYER

1 John 4:1–5; John 16:33

VERSE OF THE DAY

No, in all these things we are more than conquerors through him who loved us. —Romans 8:37

PRAYER

Lord, victory is Yours, and because I am in You, You have made me more than a conqueror. Through faith in You, I am able to overcome while living in the in-between. Thank You for giving us Jesus, who defeated sin, was raised in victory, completed the work, and is now sitting at Your right hand. When I am tempted to allow the world to overcome me and walk in a posture of defeat, remind me of Your victory over the world, so that I may walk in a posture of victory too.

THINK

PRAY

PRAISE

_____
_____
_____

TO-DO   ## PRAYER LIST

_____   _____

_____   _____

_____   _____

QUESTIONS FOR DEEPER REFLECTION

1. In what circumstances do you struggle to walk in a posture of victory?

_____
_____
_____

2. In what ways have you seen your faith help you overcome the world?

_____
_____
_____

DAY 15

GOD FAITHFULLY PROVIDES RAINBOWS

And God said, "This is the sign of the covenant that I make
between me and you and every living creature that is with you,
for all future generations: I have set my bow in the cloud, and it
shall be a sign of the covenant between me and the earth."
—Genesis 9:12–13

I was sitting in the waiting room of the intensive care unit with my friend while doctors and nurses tried to save her husband. The weather outside matched the bleak outlook inside. But as often happens in Florida, the clouds gave way to sunshine, and as the sun pierced through, the most brilliant rainbow spread across the sky above the hospital, a sign of hope in the midst of a storm.

The next day, I returned to sit and wait and pray and be present with my friend. As we sat there feeling anxious, fighting back fear and *what-ifs*, waiting for a sign of hope again, a security guard walked in with a "Get Well Soon" balloon featuring a rainbow border. He explained that he had purchased the balloon for a little boy whom he saw yesterday, but couldn't find again. So instead, he brought it to the ICU waiting room.

He told us, "You know, I saw the most beautiful rainbow over the hospital yesterday. And I just love how after the storm and the clouds clear, the rainbow comes. And this balloon just reminded me of that rainbow. I thought it would brighten someone's day."

Goosebumps crawled over my arms, and tears welled in my eyes. Hope showed up again.

In Genesis 6–9, we read the story of Noah. Corruption and sin are spreading, and God is going to destroy the earth. He calls one righteous man, Noah, to build an ark to save his family and a remnant of animals. The rains come and pour down upon the whole earth for forty days and forty nights. The land is destroyed, but Noah, his family, and the animals pass safely through the waters. Genesis 8 opens with God's breath—the same Hebrew word for *Holy Spirit*, the same word hovering over the chaos in Genesis 1—hovering over the chaotic waters again. His wind goes out, and the waters recede.

As Noah, his family, and the animals disembark, God makes a promise: never again will He flood the earth because of man's sin. In Genesis 9:12–13, God seals the covenant with a sign: a rainbow across the sky.

As a child, I remember seeing every rainbow and thinking, *There's my promise that God won't flood the earth again.* As an adult, I have come to understand that the rainbow God paints in the sky is more than a mere promise to never again kill off the entire earth. It is a promise that He will be merciful and forbearing of our sin.

Hidden in that promise is the promise of another way. The rainbow is a reminder that God in His mercy would send a Redeemer—Jesus, the Messiah and our Savior. And He faithfully fulfilled that promise. God says in Genesis 9:16, *"When the bow is in the clouds, I will see it and remember the everlasting covenant between God and every living creature of all flesh that is on the earth."* The rainbow is forever a sign that God is faithful and trustworthy.

SOMETHING TO THINK ABOUT

I love how visual our God is. He gives us physical reminders because He knows how we are prone to forget. He knew we would need help remembering.

So remember the rainbows. Remember the times hope shows up again and again. Remember the physical ways He reminds you of His faithfulness.

The outcomes may not always be what we want, but God will always be faithful. He has made an everlasting covenant of mercy with us. In the bleak circumstances and stormy seasons, His covenant will always pierce through in brilliance and beauty, reminding us that He is the God who keeps His word. Because God faithfully keeps His everlasting covenant, we can faithfully trust Him, no matter how stormy that sky may seem.

EXTRA VERSES FOR STUDY OR PRAYER

Psalm 40

VERSE OF THE DAY

And God said, "This is the sign of the covenant that I make between me and you and every living creature that is with you, for all future generations: I have set my bow in the cloud, and it shall be a sign of the covenant between me and the earth.
—Genesis 9:12–13

PRAYER

God of mercy, You are faithful to keep Your everlasting covenant with us. I will remember Your promise. When the skies are gray and the situation seems bleak, let me remember Your faithfulness, let me speak a testimony of Your faithful deeds. Your faithfulness preserves me. Help me remember the rainbows.

THINK

PRAY

_____

_____

_____

PRAISE

_____

_____

_____

TO-DO

_____

_____

_____

PRAYER LIST

_____

_____

_____

QUESTIONS FOR DEEPER REFLECTION

1. What is God's everlasting covenant with us?

_____

_____

_____

2. I am a big fan of keeping lists of times I see God remind me of His faithfulness. Use this space to record some instances where you have seen God remind you of His everlasting covenant.

_____

_____

_____

DAY 16

GOD IS FAITHFUL
TO NOT PUT YOU TO SHAME

No one who hopes in you will ever be put to shame, but shame will come on those who are treacherous without cause.
—Psalm 25:3 (NIV)

My brain is always coming up with plans: plans for the future, how I think things are going to go, and big dreams. The problem is that I often vocalize these plans with false certainty, and 99.9 percent of them never come to fruition. Shame inevitably follows.

Shame results when we fail to live up to expectations. It's the feeling of being less than, disappointing yourself or others, and it often comes when we put our trust in something not trustworthy. Shame is not from the Lord. Shame is the game of the enemy. He loves nothing more than to tempt us with sin, make the world seem more trustworthy than it is, and highlight pleasure over obedience. Then, he uses it against us. In my book *Feasting on Truth: Savor the Life-Giving Word of God,*[6] I note, "Sin always overpromises and underdelivers." The enemy knows this.

In Psalm 25, David writes an acrostic poem—each verse starts with a subsequent letter of the Hebrew alphabet—and he begins with trust:

---

6. Erin H. Warren, *Feasting on Truth: Savor the Life-Giving Word of God* (Windermere, FL: Headley Warren Productions, 2022).

*In you, Lord my God, I put my trust. I trust in you; do not let
me be put to shame, nor let my enemies triumph over me. No one
who hopes in you will ever be put to shame.*   Psalm 25:1–3 NIV

Our ability to withstand the lies of the enemy starts with our
trust in God. When we put our confidence in Him, we will never be
put to shame. Yes, the world may try to shame us or make us believe
our hope is in vain, but we must remain firmly rooted in our faith and
trust in God. We must stand firm on the solid foundation of God's
Word.

There are several ways we shore up our foundation to fight back
when the enemy tries to shame us. First, we must have a humble and
teachable spirit. We must continue to read and learn about God's
Word, knowing we will never reach an end to this knowledge. We
must recognize that we do not have the answers, but that doesn't
mean we cannot trust God. The more we learn of Him and His
Word, the surer the foundation on which we stand. Several times in
Psalm 25, David asks the Lord to teach and guide him.

*Show me your ways, Lord, teach me your paths. Guide me in
your truth and teach me, for you are God my Savior, and my
hope is in you all day long.*   Psalm 25:4–5 NIV

Being humble means admitting we cannot stand on our own. We
need Jesus to teach us. When we humbly come to Him, openhanded,
laying aside our own agendas, He will faithfully teach and guide us,
and that's the second way we shore up our foundation.

*Good and upright is the Lord; therefore he instructs sinners in
his ways. He guides the humble in what is right and teaches them
his way.*   Psalm 25:8–9 NIV

He is good. He is upright, which means He is correct and righteous. There is no flaw in Him, therefore His Word is good and ben-
eficial to us. All His ways are faithful, and we learn them through
His Word.

*All the ways of the LORD are loving and faithful toward those
who keep the demands of his covenant.*   Psalm 25:10 NIV

When we know God's faithful ways, the enemy loses his ability
to make us doubt. Using the words of Isaiah, Peter reminds us:

*As you come to him, a living stone rejected by men but in the
sight of God chosen and precious, you yourselves like living stones
are being built up as a spiritual house, to be a holy priesthood, to
offer spiritual sacrifices acceptable to God through Jesus Christ.
For it stands in Scripture: "Behold, I am laying in Zion a stone,
a cornerstone chosen and precious, and whoever believes in him
will not be put to shame."*   1 Peter 2:4–6

Believe God. Take Him at His Word. He will not be the source
of shame. Your hope is safe in Him.

SOMETHING TO THINK ABOUT

Sin may lead to shame, but our faith in God never will. Thanks
be to God! He is trustworthy through and through. Satan will try to
tell you otherwise. He will scheme and lie to make you believe God's
way is not best and that trusting in His Word is pointless, but let's put
our stake in the ground and proclaim, *"My eyes are ever on the LORD,
for only he will release my feet from the snare"* (Psalm 25:15 NIV). Let the
truth of His Word sink deep into our hearts. Let His truth protect
us: *"May integrity and uprightness protect me, because my hope, LORD,
is in you"* (Psalm 25:21 NIV). Our hope in God is not hope misplaced.

EXTRA VERSES FOR STUDY OR PRAYER

Isaiah 28:16; Romans 5:1–5; 1 Peter 2

VERSE OF THE DAY

*No one who hopes in you will ever be put to shame, but shame
will come on those who are treacherous without cause.*

—Psalm 25:3 (NIV)

PRAYER

Lord, I know that shame is not from You. Your ways are faithful and good. I humbly ask that You teach me and guide me in Your Word, so that my hope will be firmly rooted in You. When Satan comes prowling, help me stand firmly on the cornerstone of Jesus Christ and the price He paid on my behalf. Forgiveness is sure, so help me continue to trust You more each day.

THINK

_____
_____
_____

PRAY

_____
_____
_____

PRAISE

_____
_____
_____

TO-DO

_____

_____

_____

PRAYER LIST

_____

_____

_____

QUESTIONS FOR DEEPER REFLECTION

1. In what ways has the enemy tried to shame you?

_____

_____

_____

2. What Scripture verses help you fight back against the enemy's lies?

_____

_____

_____

DAY 17

GOD FAITHFULLY
GIVES ETERNAL LIFE

*For God so loved the world, that he gave his only Son, that who-
ever believes in him should not perish but have eternal life.*
—John 3:16

John 3:16. It's the most famous Bible verse in the world. We see it on posters at sporting events and graffitied along roadways. It's one of the first verses we learn as children. It is the entire gospel in one verse. But when I took the time to study this verse in context? Insert mind-blowing emoji.

One of my favorite aspects of Bible study is to see how the Old Testament ties into the New Testament. The Old Testament is a shadow, pointing us to the truth of Jesus. It's something we often miss today. We have to remember that the Jewish people were an oral society, meaning they would have memorized much of the Old Testament. That's how God preserved His Word for thousands of years. That's why there are so many verses in Scripture about teaching the Word to your children. It's literally how the next generation would learn about God. So when we see an Old Testament reference in the New Testament, for the original audience, it would have immediately triggered the hearer to recall that verse as well as the surrounding ones and then see the connection to Jesus.

That's what Jesus does here in conversation with a religious leader named Nicodemus. A Pharisee, Nicodemus comes to Jesus under the cover of night. He has questions, but the religious leaders are not exactly fans of Jesus. Nicodemus asks hard questions, and Jesus graciously gives him answers. Nicodemus knows the Torah, the first five books of the Bible, intimately. So when Jesus says, *"And as Moses lifted up the serpent in the wilderness, so must the Son of Man be lifted up, that whoever believes in him may have eternal life"* (John 3:14–15), Nicodemus would have immediately recalled the story of the bronze serpent we find in Numbers 21.

Moses and the Israelites were wandering around in the wilderness, and the people grew impatient and began to complain yet again.

> *And the people spoke against God and against Moses, "Why have you brought us up out of Egypt to die in the wilderness? For there is no food and no water, and we loathe this worthless food." Then the* LORD *sent fiery serpents among the people, and they bit the people, so that many people of Israel died.*
> Numbers 21:5–6

Each day, God was providing manna and quail for the people to eat—and they called it *worthless!* They *loathed* what the Lord had provided for them. So God sent fiery serpents, and in the face of death, the people cried out and repented. They admitted their sin and asked Moses to pray and ask God to remove the serpents. Moses prayed, and God made a way.

> *And the* LORD *said to Moses, "Make a fiery serpent and set it on a pole, and everyone who is bitten, when he sees it, shall live." So Moses made a bronze serpent and set it on a pole. And if a serpent bit anyone, he would look at the bronze serpent and live.*
> Number 21:8–9

Notice God didn't remove the serpents, but instead provided those who were bitten with a means of escaping death and finding life.

Y'all! *That* is the background of John 3:16. Jesus is drawing a connection between Numbers 21 and Himself. He is saying that, just as the people merely needed to look to the bronze serpent raised in the wilderness and find life, we merely need to look upon our Savior, believe in Him, and find *eternal* life. The serpent was lifted up to give life for the moment. Jesus was lifted up on a cross to give life forever.

SOMETHING TO THINK ABOUT

Signs reading, "John 3:16" draw a lot of attention, but the next verse gives us an important distinction for Christ's ministry:

For God did not send his Son into the world to condemn the world, but in order that the world might be saved through him.
John 3:17

Many believe that Jesus came to condemn people, but He actually came to save. Like the Israelites in the wilderness who were bitten by the serpents, we were headed for death. There was no way out. But Jesus. He stepped out of heaven and came here to do what we could not. He paid the price, so that we might be saved through Him and so receive the gift of eternal life. The Israelites had to turn their eyes to the bronze serpent. It was their choice: they could try to save themselves or trust in God's provision of salvation. We must do the same. We can put our faith in His true salvation, knowing that in Him we escape condemnation and find life forever. As we have seen His faithfulness throughout Scripture, we can trust that He will be faithful to give eternal life as well.

EXTRA VERSES FOR STUDY OR PRAYER

Numbers 21; John 8:28

VERSE OF THE DAY

For God so loved the world, that he gave his only Son, that whoever believes in him should not perish but have eternal life.
—John 3:16

PRAYER

Thank You, Jesus, for the gift of eternal life. I know that without You, I am condemned to death. But as the Israelites in the wilderness looked upon the bronze serpent to find life, so I look to You, knowing that in You, I find eternal life. When I am tempted to doubt, remind me of Your faithfulness. You will accomplish all that You say You will.

THINK

PRAY

PRAISE

TO-DO

PRAYER LIST

QUESTIONS FOR DEEPER REFLECTION

1. How does the bronze serpent in Numbers 21 give us a picture of the eternal life that Jesus provides?

---

2. What other verses in Scripture give the promise of eternal life?

DAY 18

GOD IS FAITHFUL TO STEADFASTLY LOVE YOU

Give thanks to the God of heaven, for his
steadfast love endures forever.
—Psalm 136:26

I love a good rom-com movie. My life has so much angst, but when sitting down to enjoy a romantic comedy, I find relief in the softness and joy of a good ol' love story. I've noticed over time, however, that there's a formula in rom-com storytelling: Boy meets girl. Boy and girl date. Boy and girl have misunderstanding. Musical montage of boy and girl living lives apart, pondering whether this relationship is worth it. Boy and girl ultimately reconcile to live happily ever after. This is human love—an ebb and flow, give and take, misunderstanding and reconciliation.

But this is not indicative of the steadfast love of our God.

The Hebrew word for "steadfast love" is *hesed*. You may also see it translated as "lovingkindness" or "mercy." *Hesed* is used over 250 times in the Old Testament, with 129 of those instances in Psalms alone. It's a word that is hard to define in English, but it is best described as loyal love. It refers to God's covenant loyalty to us. His love and loyalty to us are firmly fixed. This word is never used to describe people's love; it's always in reference to God's love. It is not conditional. It is not a love we earn. Steadfast love is who God is, and it endures forever.

In Exodus 34, Moses asks God to show him His glory, and the Lord does so. He hides Moses in the cleft of a rock, places His hand over the opening (because no one can see God and live), and passes before him.

> The LORD descended in the cloud and stood with him there, and proclaimed the name of the LORD. The LORD passed before him and proclaimed, "The LORD, the LORD, a God merciful and gracious, slow to anger, and abounding in steadfast love and faithfulness, keeping steadfast love for thousands, forgiving iniquity and transgression and sin, but who will by no means clear the guilty, visiting the iniquity of the fathers on the children and the children's children, to the third and the fourth generation." And Moses quickly bowed his head toward the earth and worshiped.
>
> Exodus 34:5–8

This is God's name. It is who He is. And among these verses, we find two characteristics of His steadfast love: our God is abounding and keeping. His love is not just enough or the bare minimum; His steadfast love *abounds*!

That means that you can never sin so much that He won't love you. His love for you will never diminish because of your mistakes. You're not that powerful.

His love is also kept for thousands of generations. The Hebrew word *hesed* literally means to preserve and guard with fidelity. Unlike human love, God's steadfast love is not fickle. He keeps it. He preserves His loyalty to us. I think we sometimes struggle to grasp the infinite, enduring character of God's loyal love to us. But when we do catch a glimpse, our response will be that of Moses—worship.

Psalm 136 is a psalm of praise for God's steadfast love. It is an anthem to remember His faithfulness to us. Each of the twenty-six verses end with this truth: *"For his steadfast love endures forever."*

SOMETHING TO THINK ABOUT

Notice that the psalmist begins and ends with thanksgiving. Our response to His steadfast love should be one of gratitude. I am truly humbled when I think of His steadfast love for me. I have messed up a great deal in my life, and I do not deserve this kind of love, yet He gives it to me, even when I was a sinner. (See Romans 5:8.) No matter what I do, His love will not depart from me. (See Isaiah 54:10.)

Let's come with thanksgiving before our steadfastly loving and loyal God. He is good, and He has done great things. Because His steadfast love endures forever, I can worship Him, knowing His love abounds and is kept for me.

EXTRA VERSES FOR STUDY OR PRAYER

Exodus 34; Isaiah 54:10; Romans 5:8

VERSE OF THE DAY

Give thanks to the God of heaven, for his steadfast love endures forever.   —Psalm 136:26

PRAYER

Oh, Lord, Your steadfast love endures forever. There is no end to Your covenant loyalty. Thank You for Your faithfulness in loving me not because of what I do, but because of who You are. You are good, gracious, merciful, and compassionate. Let me not use Your love as a cover for sin, but let it compel me toward holiness. Let my life be a song of worship because of Your enduring *hesed*.

THINK

PRAY

_____

_____

_____

PRAISE

_____

_____

_____

TO-DO   PRAYER LIST

_____   _____

_____   _____

_____   _____

QUESTIONS FOR DEEPER REFLECTION

1. What keeps you from believing God's love for you is steadfast?

_____

_____

_____

2. Like the psalmist in Psalm 136, list some specific ways you have seen God's faithfulness affirm His steadfast love for you.

_____

_____

_____

DAY 19

GOD FAITHFULLY
GIVES HOPE

*We have this as a sure and steadfast anchor of the soul, a hope
that enters into the inner place behind the curtain.*
—Hebrews 6:19

Hope is a word that has thrown me for many years. I would read about hope in Scripture, but it didn't match my twenty-first century English definition of hope. We throw this word around a great deal: "I hope my team wins the game." "I hope my kids don't fuss about the Brussels sprouts." "I hope I get the job." "I hope there's no traffic on my commute."

This hope has the potential for various outcomes—some favorable, some not-so-favorable. It's my way of saying what I want to happen while acknowledging that it may not happen. So when I read about putting hope in God, or the fact that my hope in God is secure, I was confused. Hope isn't something sure in today's world. So what is this sure hope that God gives?

Hope in the ancient world meant something much deeper than our understanding of it today. Hope was synonymous with trust. In fact, you can replace the word "hope" with "trust" in most verses. This gives us a clearer picture of the hope that God faithfully gives us.

In Hebrews 6, the author uses the example of God's covenant with Abraham, where He promised to make Abraham a great nation, to convey the idea of this sure hope we have in Him. He says:

For people swear by something greater than themselves, and in all their disputes an oath is final for confirmation. So when God desired to show more convincingly to the heirs of the promise the unchangeable character of his purpose, he guaranteed it with an oath, so that by two unchangeable things, in which it is impossible for God to lie, we who have fled for refuge might have strong encouragement to hold fast to the hope set before us.

Hebrews 6:16–18

God made an oath to confirm the covenant He had made with Abraham, and since God is unchangeable and His character is unchangeable, the promise is unchangeable. The promise stands because God cannot lie. The book of Hebrews is written to Jewish believers who are not only facing persecution from the government, but also being cast out of synagogues and even their own families for believing in Jesus. Their life circumstances are causing them to question their faith, but the author of Hebrews writes to encourage them to hold fast to the hope set before them. God is sure; therefore, He gives a hope that is sure and steadfast: Jesus.

Jesus is our Hope. He is our Great High Priest who entered the most holy place, offering the sacrifice of His own blood on our behalf. The curtain that divided the people from God's presence tore in two when Jesus breathed His last on the cross. (See Matthew 27:51.) Now we have access to God Himself. This is the hope that anchors our souls.

SOMETHING TO THINK ABOUT

An anchor holds a boat in place so that it doesn't drift away in a storm or with the normal movement of water. The hope that we have does the same. When life's storms threaten to toss us to and fro, take us off course, or make us lose our way, we remember that God faithfully gives us hope, a firm trust that He is who says He is and does what He says He will. This hope is sure and steadfast. It's firm, reliable, trustworthy, and certain. It's enduring, stable, and unshakable.

Hold it. Don't let it go. Because God faithfully gives hope, trust Him and stay the course of faith.

EXTRA VERSES FOR STUDY OR PRAYER

Romans 5:1–5; Colossians 1:21–29

VERSE OF THE DAY

We have this as a sure and steadfast anchor of the soul, a hope that enters into the inner place behind the curtain.
—Hebrews 6:19

PRAYER

You are the God who faithfully gives hope. You are trustworthy and true, so I know I can put my full hope, my full trust, my full confidence, and my full faith in You. Hope in You will never lead to shame. When the storms threaten to throw my faith off course, help me remember to drop anchor, remaining sure and steadfast as I trust in You.

THINK

PRAY

PRAISE

TO-DO   PRAYER LIST

....

....

....

QUESTIONS FOR DEEPER REFLECTION

1. How does knowing hope is synonymous with trust change your understanding of the sure hope spoken of in Scripture?

....

....

....

2. In what areas of your life do you need to drop anchor and remember God's trustworthy hope?

....

....

....

DAY 20

GOD FAITHFULLY
GIVES STRENGTH

*He gives power to the faint, and to him who has no might he
increases strength. Even youths shall faint and be weary, and young
men shall fall exhausted; but they who wait for the LORD shall
renew their strength; they shall mount up with wings like eagles;
they shall run and not be weary; they shall walk and not faint.*
—Isaiah 40:29–31

A few years ago, I had pain in my shoulder that affected my sleep and my ability to drive. I could barely hold anything on my right side. After some tests, my doctor told me that I have hyperlaxity syndrome or extra stretchy ligaments, meaning I was generally unstable. (Go ahead, laugh. I totally did!) The ligaments that hold my bones together are more flexible than they should be, which makes it harder for my joints to stay in place. The remedy? I needed to build up my muscles. I needed more strength in order to be more stable. (Still laughing.) After some physical therapy and adjustments to my workout routine, the problem eventually dissipated.

Our faith works the same way. In order to be more stable and steadfast in our faith, we need to build our spiritual muscles. The good news is that we are not working out in our own strength. God Himself gives us His. He is our stability and source of strength.

In Isaiah 40, we see a progression of thoughts from the prophet that are clearly not a coincidence. The chapter opens with God's comfort, helping us remember that in our pain, He provides the abundant comfort we need. He does this through His faithful word. (See Isaiah 40:8.) Therefore, we praise Him because He is great and mighty (verse 10) and tends to His flock (verse 11). Who can measure Him (vv. 12–13)? Who is His counselor (v. 14)? Who can say that they *"taught him knowledge, and showed him the way of understanding?"* (Isaiah 40:14). Who can compare to Him (v. 18)? No one. Only He is mighty and strong in power (v. 26).

My strength is no match for God's. Without Him, I am unstable and prone to fear. But He is with me; therefore, I have strength.

SOMETHING TO THINK ABOUT

Most days, I'm very tired, weighed down by lack of sleep and the stress of having a child with a chronic medical condition. But I've learned that when I'm weak, I'm better poised to recognize my limitations. They cause me to rely on God's strength more than my own. And, praise God, His strength never runs out, because He is the everlasting God. (See Isaiah 40:28–31.)

He alone is the Creator of the whole earth. He alone is mighty and powerful. He alone is the everlasting, eternal, and infinite God. He never gets tired. He never grows weary. He never works Himself too hard. We are finite. Our strength is finite. Our energy is finite. Our resources are finite. Even my kids, who seem to have everlasting energy, eventually grow tired and give way to sleep.

But not our God.

He gives us His strength to keep running the race. He gives us the power to face the day. Because God faithfully gives me strength, I can put my full dependence on Him, the everlasting power source.

EXTRA VERSES FOR STUDY OR PRAYER

Psalm 29; Isaiah 40:28–31

VERSE OF THE DAY

He gives power to the faint, and to him who has no might he increases strength. Even youths shall faint and be weary, and young men shall fall exhausted; but they who wait for the LORD shall renew their strength; they shall mount up with wings like eagles; they shall run and not be weary; they shall walk and not faint. —Isaiah 40:29–31

PRAYER

God, I am tired. Some days my faith feels unstable as I am powerless in the face of the challenges of my day. But You are the everlasting God, therefore, I do not need to fear. You give strength and power through Your presence. Let me continue to rely fully on You, the Source of all I need to face the day.

THINK

_____

_____

_____

PRAY

_____

_____

_____

PRAISE

_____

_____

_____

TO-DO   PRAYER LIST

_____   _____

_____   _____

_____   _____

QUESTIONS FOR DEEPER REFLECTION

1. What is making you weary right now?

_____

_____

_____

2. What other verses in Scripture remind you that God is the Source of all we need?

_____

_____

_____

DAY 21

GOD FAITHFULLY SUSTAINS US

I lay down and slept; I woke again, for the LORD sustained me.
—Psalm 3:5

I'm kind of a klutz. I blame it on my small feet; I'm one inch shy of six feet tall and wear a size 6.5 shoe. (I know. It's ridiculous.) Remember how I'm unstable? (Yes, still laughing.) I could entertain you for hours with stories of how I've fallen, or run into things and embarrassed myself. (Brooke and I commiserate over this "talent.") Y'all, one time I somehow ran into a door and sprained my ankle. You can't make this stuff up. Another time, I stepped off a curb wrong and twisted that same ankle pretty badly. That time, I ended up on crutches. I could not put any weight on my foot and needed support in order to walk.

My clumsiness is a great metaphor for our walk with God. We cannot do it alone; we need His support.

In 2 Samuel 15, we find King David fleeing from his son, Absalom. Absalom is a bad dude who's trying to overthrow his father as king. Upon hearing that Absalom is headed for Jerusalem, David tells his servants and his entire household to flee the city before Absalom arrives and kills them all. As they leave, King David climbs the Mount of Olives, *"weeping as he went, barefoot and with his head covered"* (2 Samuel 15:30).

I imagine David prayed Psalm 3 through those tears. The odds are stacked against him, but his faith in God does not waiver. He reminds himself of the character of His God—that He is a shield and *"the lifter of my head"* (Psalm 3:3). I love that imagery. In the midst of fear as the enemy closes in, David does something unexpected: he sleeps and he wakes, knowing it was the Lord who sustained him.

The Hebrew word for *sustained* means to lean, lay, rest, or support. Like I needed to lean on the crutches in order to walk, we can lean on God for the support we need as we walk through hardship or fear that the enemy is closing in. We can rest on Him, and He carries us. When we recognize that He alone sustains us, fear gives way to confidence—confidence that allows us to rest.

SOMETHING TO THINK ABOUT

Trusting in ourselves nets us nothing. God says in Jeremiah, *"Cursed is the man who trusts in man and makes his flesh his strength, whose heart turns away from the* Lord*"* (Jeremiah 17:5). Such a person will live *"in the parched places"* (verse 6), and no good will come to him. But I love the contrast for the one who trusts in the Lord.

> *Blessed is the man who trusts in the* Lord*, whose trust is the* Lord*. He is like a tree planted by water, that sends out its roots by the stream, and does not fear when heat comes, for its leaves remain green, and is not anxious in the year of drought, for it does not cease to bear fruit.*   Jeremiah 17:7–8

When we trust in the Lord, when our trust *is* the Lord, we will be like a tree planted by streams of water, a constant flow of nourishment reaching down to its roots. He sustains us when we remain in Him, and the result is a faith that does not whither or become fearful when things heat up, or grow anxious when supplies seem to dwindle. Instead, we will continue to be upright, sustained, and supported, bearing the fruit of faith that only comes through putting the full weight of our trust in our sustaining God. Because God is faithful to sustain me, I can rest fully on Him.

EXTRA VERSES FOR STUDY OR PRAYER

Jeremiah 17:5–9

VERSE OF THE DAY

I lay down and slept; I woke again, for the Lord sustained me.
—Psalm 3:5

PRAYER

Lord, my trust is not in myself or anything of the flesh. I put the full weight of my faith on Your sustaining promise. Let me remember Your faithfulness when the heat threatens to destroy, or the drought causes me to think I do not have enough. You are the God who sustains me, and I trust You.

THINK

PRAY

PRAISE

TO-DO   PRAYER LIST

_____   _____

_____   _____

_____   _____

QUESTIONS FOR DEEPER REFLECTION

1. Read Jeremiah 17:5–9. What is the difference between those who put their trust in people versus those who put their trust in God?

_____

_____

_____

2. In what areas of life do you need to lean on the Lord, trusting Him to sustain and support you?

_____

_____

_____

DAY 22

GOD FAITHFULLY GUIDES US

I will instruct you and teach you in the way you should go; I will counsel you with my eye upon you.
—Psalm 32:8

I am directionally challenged. Do not tell me to turn north or go east on the highway. If you're driving and ask me if you need to turn right or left, I will pause and look at my hands. I will think to myself, *I write with this hand and that's the way to turn.* Then I will look at you and say, "Turn right." I struggle getting my bearings and knowing which way to go. When I used to travel for work, pre-GPS, I would always go to a map website and print directions for all the routes I had to drive—the airport to the hotel, the hotel to the meeting location, the location to the restaurant for dinner… I got lost several times!

Thank goodness technology has evolved and directions are now at our fingertips at all times. I have a pleasant Australian accent telling me which way to go, and it's getting more and more accurate. It relieves the stress of feeling like we might get lost. My GPS gives me confidence to move forward, knowing its guidance will get me where I need to go.

God promises to guide us, but His guidance is on a whole other level. Yes, there are times that God gives us specific physical directions, but the older I get and the longer I follow Jesus, the more I feel like God's direction is less about where we go and what we do;

instead, it's about who we are. There are several passages in Scripture that reiterate God's promise to guide us, but I love the imagery David uses in Psalm 32. He draws an important distinction for us in the way God guides us.

> *I will instruct you and teach you in the way you should go; I will counsel you with my eye upon you. Be not like a horse or a mule, without understanding, which must be curbed with bit and bridle, or it will not stay near you.*   Psalm 32:8–9

A trained horse or mule allows itself to be controlled without needing to understand where it's going, kind of like me following my GPS. But when the bridle is removed, the animal takes off aimlessly. The horse runs aimlessly. God does not want us to be blindly controlled, but rather He teaches and trains us in His way so we follow wisely.

Scripture often uses the imagery of walking on a path or following *the way* when it talks about how we should live. On the surface, it seems like a physical path, but it is a metaphor for a spiritual journey. As I shared in my book *Feasting on Truth*, the Bible "is not a book meant to guide our every whim; it is a book God uses to guide us to Himself."[7] We so often look at Scripture as a guidebook for life on earth, looking for answers to our questions, when, truly, it's a book that teaches us the character of God and how we should live in light of who He is.

It was such a relief for me to realize that God walks with us and guides us as we go. Remember how He is a caring shepherd? He guides us to Himself, and as He makes us more like Himself, He equips us with wisdom and discernment to navigate life here on earth.

SOMETHING TO THINK ABOUT

I may not be great with north and south, right and left, but I am good with landmarks. My brain immediately comprehends "go toward downtown" or "turn at the grocery store." So as you are

7. Warren, *Feasting on Truth*.

looking for guidance in your life, go toward Jesus. Which physical path is going to align with His Word? God does not hide from you. He is plainly found, especially in His Word. God says, *"Draw near to me, hear this: from the beginning I have not spoken in secret, from the time it came to be I have been there"* (Isaiah 48:16). Know that His goal is for you to be more like Him and less like the world.

He desires us to grow in wisdom and discernment. He has given us His Word, and He has given us a personal guide, the Holy Spirit, for knowing and understanding truth. (See John 16:13.)

Not sure which direction to take? Go toward Jesus. Draw near to Him, and He will guide you in the way.

EXTRA VERSES FOR STUDY OR PRAYER

Psalm 73:23–26; Psalm 119:105; Isaiah 48:16; John 16:13

VERSE OF THE DAY

I will instruct you and teach you in the way you should go; I will counsel you with my eye upon you. —Psalm 32:8

PRAYER

God, You are the Good Shepherd who guides Your people, and You guide us to Yourself. I do not have all the answers, but You are the all-knowing God. Teach me and counsel me. Let my heart be teachable as I grow in understanding. Let me see more of You today as Your Holy Spirit guides me toward truth.

THINK

_____

_____

_____

PRAY

PRAISE

TO-DO

PRAYER LIST

QUESTIONS FOR DEEPER REFLECTION

1. How does knowing God's guidance is more about leading you to Himself than to a specific destination shift the way you think of God's promise to guide you?

2. Where in your life have you seen God grow you in wisdom and discernment?

DAY 23

GOD FAITHFULLY
GIVES JOY

So also you have sorrow now, but I will see you again, and your
hearts will rejoice, and no one will take your joy from you.
—John 16:22

Joy is a promise. But goodness, there are times when joy is hard fought. Psalm 16:11 tells us that in God's *"presence there is fullness of joy,"* but when the heat rises and the pressure intensifies, it's hard to cling to this promise.

We visited the end of John:16 on Day 8. Now, I want us to focus on another truth from this chapter: because God is faithful in suffering, we can have coming, lasting, and complete joy.

God faithfully gives us joy, both now and for eternity. I believe Jesus has a twofold meaning when He speaks these words. The immediate meaning is that in just a matter of hours, Jesus will be arrested, tried, and crucified, and His followers will be devastated. But I believe He is also talking about eternity. He likens it to childbirth, which is often used in Scripture as an example of the painful wait for the Messiah and the second coming. (See Romans 8:22–24; John 16:21.) Jesus tells them joy is coming—in the short term, when He walks out of that grave, but also in the long term, when He comes back to claim His bride. I feel this angst almost daily in our world as I watch those around us rejoicing over their own sin, while we mourn that this isn't how life should be. But joy is coming! The joy the world offers is temporary; it won't satisfy and ultimately leads to death. (See Romans 6:20–21.) But for those who put their trust and confidence in Jesus, the mourning is temporary. Joy is coming.

> *Truly, truly, I say to you, you will weep and lament, but the world will rejoice. You will be sorrowful, but your sorrow will turn into joy.* John 16:20

God gives us a lasting joy. Satan would love nothing more than to steal our joy, but the joy we have because of Jesus cannot be taken from us.

When my oldest was about two years old, I embarked on a brave day of errands in the rain. It was one of those days when it just rained all day, but I was determined to check things off my list. After we were done, I wanted to take my son to my favorite bakery as a reward. When we walked in, my son immediately turned around, climbed up on a chair, and stared out the window at the rain and puddles. I called out several times, "Turn around! Look at all the treats!" But he wouldn't take his eyes off the rain. The ladies behind the counter were laughing as this exchange went on for several minutes. Despite all the times I told him of the goodness waiting if he'd just turn around and look, he only wanted to see the rain.

God convicted my heart that day. Sometimes we are so focused on the rain, puddles, and hard stuff in our lives that we miss the blessing God has for us if we'll just turn around. He is saying, "Turn around! I have all these promises for you! You simply have to take hold of them." When we put our faith in Christ and the Holy Spirit comes to live in us, He brings the most wonderful gift: the fruit of the Spirit. (See Galatians 5:22–23.) Joy is one of those fruits!

SOMETHING TO THINK ABOUT

The joy we get in Christ is complete—not lacking, not defective, not in process. We get all of it, all at once.

> *Until now you have asked nothing in my name. Ask, and you will receive, that your joy may be full.* John 16:24

I know this sounds good, but how do we take hold of this coming, lasting, complete joy? Jesus tells us, *"I am the vine; you are the branches. Whoever abides in me and I in him, he it is that bears much fruit, for apart from me you can do nothing"* (John 15:5). We will bear the fruit of joy when we remain in Him and abide in His Word. We will not experience this joy apart from God.

When you need to be reminded of His joy, turn around and look to His Word. Remember His faithfulness. Remember His character. Remember His promises. Remember that only in Him will you find the joy that can exist even in the face of darkness. *"These things I have spoken to you, that my joy may be in you, and that your joy may be full"* (John 15:11).

EXTRA VERSES FOR STUDY OR PRAYER

Psalm 16; John 15; Galatians 5:22–23

VERSE OF THE DAY

So also you have sorrow now, but I will see you again, and your hearts will rejoice, and no one will take your joy from you.

—John 16:22

PRAYER

You are the God of all joy. When my life feels anything but joyful, I can still have full joy because Your joy is in me. You are with me and in me. You have taught me in Psalm 16:9, *"Therefore my heart is glad, and my whole being rejoices."* Satan cannot take Your joy from me, so I cling to Your faithful joy.

THINK

PRAY

_____

_____

_____

PRAISE

_____

_____

_____

TO-DO

_____

_____

_____

PRAYER LIST

_____

_____

_____

QUESTIONS FOR DEEPER REFLECTION

1. What are ways that you can abide in Jesus?

_____

_____

_____

2. How does knowing God, His Word, and His character instill joy in you?

_____

_____

_____

DAY 24

GOD FAITHFULLY
GIVES NEW LIFE

We were buried therefore with him by baptism into death, in
order that, just as Christ was raised from the dead by the glory
of the Father, we too might walk in newness of life.
—Romans 6:4

As I sit here writing, I have another window open on my computer to a live feed of an incubator for baby chicks at my kids' school. We are on chick watch! My daughter and I watched two hatch last night; this morning, we began to see another one peck cracks in its egg. And then the third chick came out of its shell! I can't take my eyes off it! I'm mesmerized watching these little baby chicks come into the world. I watch as they stumble around, trying to get their footing, feathers matted by the moist environment inside their eggshells. But in a matter of a few short hours, they are walking around boldly, so fluffy and so cute! (It's a lot of exclamation points, but watching this new life is so so exciting!)

We too have new life. There are many verses in Scripture that point to new life in Christ—because God is a life-giver!

But God, who is rich in mercy, because of his great love that he
had for us, made us alive with Christ even though we were dead
in trespasses. You are saved by grace! Ephesians 2:4–5 CSB

> *Therefore, if anyone is in Christ, he is a new creation. The old has passed away; behold, the new has come!*   2 Corinthians 5:17

> *And you, who were dead in your trespasses and the uncircumcision of your flesh, God made alive together with him, having forgiven us all our trespasses.*   Colossians 2:13

I want to shout this news from the rooftops! I want to exclaim with all the exclamation points, "I was dead, but now I am alive!" Right from the beginning, in Genesis 1, we see how God creates new life, but honestly, I have wrestled with this truth. Where is my *new life* when life here on earth leaves me feeling lifeless?

The Greek word for *life* is *zóé*.[8] It embodies the concept that life is derived from a source. So what is this life we have because of Jesus? "It always (only) comes from and is sustained by *God's self-existent life*. The Lord *intimately shares* His gift of life with *people*, creating each in *His image* which gives all the capacity to know His eternal life."[9] God is the source of life because He is self-existing; He does not need anything or anyone to sustain His life. He *is* life, but He also *gives* life. His life sustains us, both physically and spiritually. His life is not *just enough* to help us get by. John 10:10 tells that He came not only to give us life, but to give it abundantly. All throughout Scripture, we see evidence of God breathing life to make what was once dead alive.

SOMETHING TO THINK ABOUT

What is fascinating to me is that the verses that follow the ones I quoted earlier all point to a similar theme: our new life in Christ affects the way we live. When we recognize the life we have because of Jesus, the way we walk will look different too. We no longer live in sin. In fact, *"sin will have no dominion"* over us (Romans 6:14). Sin does not get a say anymore. Our flesh does not control us, so we are able to take part in a process called *sanctification*. I know, it's a big word, but it's the process of looking less like our old sinful selves and, over time, looking more like Jesus.

---

8. 2222, zóé, *Strong's Greek Concordance.*
9. "2222 zōé – life," Bible Hub, biblehub.com/greek/2222.htm.

Like those newborn chicks, we will stumble as we take the first few steps of our new life, but the longer we walk with God, the steadier we become. Again, not in our own strength, but in His *zóé*.

Because God gives life, sin no longer has control over you. You can walk in His ways and lean on your sustaining God. Rejoice in your newness of life! You were once dead, but now, because of Jesus, you are alive! (Oh, and so are two more little chicks!)

EXTRA VERSES FOR STUDY OR PRAYER

John 10:10; 2 Corinthians 5:17–19; Ephesians 2:4–10; Colossians 2:8–14

VERSE OF THE DAY

We were buried therefore with him by baptism into death, in order that, just as Christ was raised from the dead by the glory of the Father, we too might walk in newness of life.

—Romans 6:4

PRAYER

Lord, You are the life-giver. You are the self-existing One who shares Your life with us. When life here leaves me feeling life-less, let me remember Your *zóé*. When I'm tempted to turn back to my old self, remind me that I am a new creation. The old has gone, and the new has come. You are faithful to give life!

THINK

PRAY

_____

_____

_____

PRAISE

_____

_____

_____

TO-DO

_____

_____

_____

PRAYER LIST

_____

_____

_____

QUESTIONS FOR DEEPER REFLECTION

1. In what areas of your life are you leaning on God's sustaining life?

_____

_____

_____

2. In what areas do you continue to try to turn back to your old self? How can you trust in God's new life for you?

_____

_____

_____

DAY 25

GOD FAITHFULLY
GIVES FREEDOM

For freedom Christ has set us free; stand firm therefore, and do
not submit again to a yoke of slavery.
—Galatians 5:1

I grew up with some good rules—I just didn't know it. One of my parents' rules was that we could only have one sweet treat per day. They wanted to teach us to have a healthy balance in our diet, but boy, was that hard for a sugar-crazed kid. I *love* sweets. So when I moved into my first apartment in college, I went a little wild. Each week, I would buy a roll of cookie dough to snack on, I drank sodas, and I would go through a pint of ice cream—on *top* of all the other unhealthy foods I was eating. I wasn't living under the same rules anymore. I was free...or so I thought.

It didn't take long for my pants to start getting a little snug, and then not fit at all. I realized that the rules my parents had put in place were wise ones. While I was no longer living under their rules, they were still good guidelines to help me live a healthy life.

The Israelites had lived under the law for centuries, but time and time again, they failed to keep it. Not one person was able to live the perfect life, fulfilling every requirement needed to live in God's presence, which is why God gave them the law to begin with. God's rules always prove that we cannot do what is required to save ourselves. We are incapable of keeping His laws and living a perfect life. The weight of that is too heavy a burden for us to bear, so God came here in the flesh, to live the perfect life and die on our behalf.

Because of Jesus, God the Son, you are free. You no longer live under the weight of the law. The price has been paid.

Under the law, we were slaves to sin. In our verse for today, Paul writes to the church of Galatia, urging them to keep walking in their freedom instead of turning back to the slavery they experienced under sin. He wanted them to stand firm in their faith, remembering they had been set free. He urged them not to sin as they had before they followed Jesus, to remember that they were new creations!

God wants the same things for us.

SOMETHING TO THINK ABOUT

Paul moves through an interesting thought pattern in Galatians 5. He starts with an argument over freedom *from* the law versus living *under* the law. Like I did when I experienced freedom in college, our tendency is to respond, "The law is dead, and we live under the grace and freedom of Christ." But as Paul continues, he points out that the law was never meant to save us. Only faith in Jesus will save us. However, in our freedom, and because we're so grateful for the work of Christ in us, we *obey* the law. Like walking in newness of life, walking in freedom affects the way we live. Paul says we do not serve ourselves; instead, we love and serve one another. The key to loving your neighbor and walking in freedom is found by walking in the Spirit.

> *But I say, walk by the Spirit, and you will not gratify the desires of the flesh. For the desires of the flesh are against the Spirit, and the desires of the Spirit are against the flesh, for these are opposed to each other, to keep you from doing the things you want to do.*
> Galatians 5:16–17

If we walk in the Spirit, allowing the Holy Spirit in us to empower us, the things of this world will lose their appeal, and we will bear the fruit of the Spirit. And what is the fruit of this life in the Spirit? It's made up of *"love, joy, peace, patience, kindness, goodness, faithfulness, gentleness, self-control"* (Galatians 5:22–23).

Living in freedom under grace gives us access to this wonderful fruit. It's all inside of us because we belong to Jesus. If we walk in the Spirit, we won't have to worry about the law because the Spirit perfectly fulfills the law. What grace! We no longer have the pressure of the law weighing us down. Because we walk in faithful freedom, we can walk in step with the Spirit and His abundant fruit.

EXTRA VERSES FOR STUDY OR PRAYER

Leviticus 19:9–18

VERSE OF THE DAY

For freedom Christ has set us free; stand firm therefore, and do not submit again to a yoke of slavery.   —Galatians 5:1

PRAYER

Father, You are the God of freedom. You fulfilled the righteous requirement of the law in Jesus, and now the weight of the law no longer rests on me. Thank You for giving us the Spirit as our Helper. I pray that You will help me keep in step with the Spirit so that I can live out the desires of the Spirit, putting to death the desires of my flesh. Help me be filled with all love, joy, peace, patience, kindness, goodness, faithfulness, gentleness, and self-control.

THINK

PRAY

_____

_____

_____

PRAISE

_____

_____

_____

TO-DO   # PRAYER LIST

_____   _____

_____   _____

_____   _____

QUESTIONS FOR DEEPER REFLECTION

1. In what areas of your life are you tempted to turn back to your old self?

_____

_____

_____

2. How does the freedom God gives you affect the way you live?

_____

_____

_____

DAY 26

GOD IS FAITHFUL TO USE HIS WORD

Your word is a lamp to my feet and a light to my path.
—Psalm 119:105

I haven't always loved reading my Bible. In fact, for most of my life, my Bible reading was nonexistent. Sure, I'd read verses here and there, but my consumption of Scripture was mostly through devotionals and fill-in-the-blank Bible studies. While these books certainly have their place—I mean, you *are* reading a devotional right now!—they will never do for you what direct study of God's Word will do for you. His Word has purpose, and God is faithful to use His Word in so many ways.

Psalm 119 is the longest chapter in the Bible, measuring in at 176 verses. (Bonus points if you read the whole thing today!) This love letter to God's Word is an acrostic poem, meaning each stanza begins with a subsequent letter of the Hebrew alphabet. A few years ago, I wrote an inductive study on Psalm 119 called *Light & Life*, and one of its focuses is discovering the ways in which God uses His Word in our lives. I give this example in the study's introduction:

Psalm 119:130 says, *"The unfolding of your words gives light; it imparts understanding to the simple."* The Hebrew word for *unfolding* means "opening or entrance." Think of His Word as a doorway. When we open His Word, it's like opening a door. The light spills out and through it, we enter into His glorious presence, where He gives us understanding, no matter how *simple* we are.[10]

Here are some of my favorite ways God uses His Word in Psalm 119:

- His Word keeps us pure: *"How can a young man keep his way pure? By guarding it according to your word"* (verse 9).

- His Word gives us strength: *"My soul melts away for sorrow; strengthen me according to your word!"* (verse 28).

- His Word gives us comfort and life: *"This is my comfort in my affliction, that your promise gives me life"* (verse 50).

- His Word leads to worship: *"At midnight I rise to praise you, because of your righteous rules"* (verse 62).

- His Word reinforces His faithfulness: *"Forever, O LORD, your word is firmly fixed in the heavens. Your faithfulness endures to all generations; you have established the earth, and it stands fast"* (verses 89–90).

- His Word points us to truth: *"Through your precepts I get understanding; therefore I hate every false way"* (verse 104).

- His Word guides us: *"Your word is a lamp to my feet and a light to my path"* (verse 105).

- His Word gives us peace and keeps us from stumbling: *"Great peace have those who love your law; nothing can make them stumble"* (verse 165).

Any time we come to Scripture, laying aside our own agendas and humbly seeking God first and foremost, He will faithfully use His Word.

SOMETHING TO THINK ABOUT

Isaiah uses beautiful imagery to explain how God uses His Word:

---

10. Erin H. Warren, *Light & Life: An Inductive Study on Psalm 119* (Orlando, FL: Headley Warren Productions, 2021).

For as the rain and the snow come down from heaven and do not return there but water the earth, making it bring forth and sprout, giving seed to the sower and bread to the eater, so shall my word be that goes out from my mouth; it shall not return to me empty, but it shall accomplish that which I purpose, and shall succeed in the thing for which I sent it.   Isaiah 55:10–11

Rain falls on the earth, soaks into the ground, nourishes the plants, and brings a harvest. Likewise, God's Word falls on us, sinks deep, nourishes our souls with truth, and brings life. We can trust that every time we open our Bibles, God is sowing seeds and watering them to bring life to our weary souls. Because God faithfully accomplishes a purpose through His Word, we can make time to read our Bibles and trust that God will build our faith.

EXTRA VERSES FOR STUDY OR PRAYER

Isaiah 55:10–11

VERSE OF THE DAY

Your word is a lamp to my feet and a light to my path.
                                        —Psalm 119:105

PRAYER

God, You are faithful to use Your Word to bring me life. As I open my Bible today, I ask that Your Holy Spirit meet me in the pages of Scripture and pour forth life-giving truths. Give me understanding, light my path, and deepen my faith as I study Your holy Word.

THINK

PRAY

_____

_____

_____

PRAISE

_____

_____

_____

TO-DO   ## PRAYER LIST

_____   _____

_____   _____

_____   _____

QUESTIONS FOR DEEPER REFLECTION

1. What other ways does God use His Word according to Psalm 119?

_____

_____

2. In what ways have you seen God use the truths of Scripture to build your faith?

_____

_____

_____

DAY 27

GOD IS FAITHFUL
TO RESTORE US

Create in me a clean heart,
O God, and renew a right spirit within me.
—Psalm 51:10

I stood there in disbelief, looking at the permanent mark on my black and white sofa. My good sofa, which "no children are ever allowed on or near," had six black squiggly lines on it. I had all of the emotions—sadness, anger, and frustration. On the one hand, I thought, *It's just a couch. It still functions. People can still sit on it.* But on the other hand, I knew that in the split moment when my little toddler somehow got hold of a permanent marker and made an art piece of my sofa, its value was completely lost. No longer would it be seen as the beautiful sofa that it had been. It was tarnished.

We sometimes see ourselves that way. We look at the black lines of marker across our lives, and we let Satan tell us we are tarnished—that God could never get the stain out, and He will never allow us to be used now. We are beyond restoration.

But nothing could be further from the truth.

Psalm 51 is a cry from King David. He has recognized his behavior with Bathsheba as sin. (See 2 Samuel 11–12.) The prophet Nathan has confronted David, and David has seen his own sin through God's eyes. He is crushed. He writes this psalm in which he begs for mercy and asks God to cleanse him from his sin.

*Purge me with hyssop, and I shall be clean; wash me, and I shall
be whiter than snow. Let me hear joy and gladness; let the bones
that you have broken rejoice. Hide your face from my sins, and
blot out all my iniquities. Create in me a clean heart, O God, and
renew a right spirit within me.* Psalm 51:7–10

David knows that God is the ultimate master of stain removal.
He claims this promise that God will cleanse and renew him.

Just as God met David where he was, God meets us where we
are—broken, bruised, tarnished, and stained—and He cleanses us
with the blood of Jesus. He renews and restores us.

Sin brings separation in our relationship with God, but His
mercy is far more abundant than our sin. He not only cleanses us,
but He faithfully restores us. (See 1 Peter 5:10.) I like to think of restoration as an additive—that He will give us more—but the Greek
word for *restore* used in 1 Peter 5:10 literally translates "to adjust
down to fully functioning." God strips away that which keeps us from
operating out of the joy of our salvation. He removes the impurities,
the sin, the marks of ink, with the goal of making us His fully functioning followers.

SOMETHING TO THINK ABOUT

God does something even more remarkable than restoring us: He
uses His restoration as part of our testimony. His cleansing renews
the joy of our salvation, and He brings glory to His name because of
it. (See Psalm 51:13–15.)

Your sin is not more powerful than God's mercy. In Him, you
will find abundant mercy that will cleanse you whiter than snow.
The churchy word for it is *justification*. It's as if you had never sinned.
That is our restoring God. So tell of His greatness! Let your lips sing
praise!

EXTRA VERSES FOR STUDY OR PRAYER

First Peter 5:10; Revelation 2:11

VERSE OF THE DAY

Create in me a clean heart, O God, and renew a right spirit within me. —Psalm 51:10

PRAYER

God, You faithfully restore the heart of the one who puts their faith in You. I have sinned. I have messed up. I am marred by sin, but You are faithful to wash me white as snow. Cleanse me and restore to me the joy of my salvation. Let me tell of Your salvation and declare Your praise. Let others turn to You because of the word of my testimony.

THINK

PRAY

PRAISE

TO-DO

PRAYER LIST

_____   _____

_____   _____

_____   _____

QUESTIONS FOR DEEPER REFLECTION

1. Where do you need God's restoration in your life?

_____

_____

_____

2. How have you seen God wash you and renew you despite your sin?

_____

_____

_____

DAY 28

GOD IS
FAITHFULLY WORTHY

O Lord, our Lord, how majestic is your name in all the earth!
—Psalm 8:9

I get lost in my thoughts a lot while I'm driving, probably because being alone in my car is pretty much the only time I'm in silence. (And truthfully, it's not all that silent!) Sometimes that is good, and sometimes that is not so good. Today, I was pondering how hard life has been. It's my daughter's birthday, but it has also been one year since my son received his type 1 diabetes diagnosis. I have a lot of thoughts about that.

My thoughts drifted to church. This past Sunday, we sang a song about magnifying the name of God, something we often do. While sitting in the pews in church on Sunday, we sing of the majesty of our God and His matchless glory. We welcome the Holy Spirit into this place of worship. He is worthy of all praise as the voices of His church rise together. But the praise and glory of our God is not reserved for Sunday sanctuaries.

As I drove, I thought, *Even here. Isn't He worthy even here in this place? Isn't He magnified here in this place? This place of grief? This place of the mundane? This place of the unknown? This place of lost dreams? This place of disappointment? This place of sickness? This place of exhaustion? This place of fear? This place of unsettledness? Isn't He still worthy?*

Yes. He is.

SOMETHING TO THINK ABOUT

Psalm 8 is a song of praise to the majestic name of God. Nothing puts me in my place faster than when I consider the greatness of God.

When I look at your heavens, the work of your fingers, the moon and the stars, which you have set in place, what is man that you are mindful of him, and the son of man that you care for him?
—Psalm 8:3–4

One does not have to look far to see the greatness of God on display. He is the Creator of all the earth, and the heavens and all of creation bow to His sovereignty. His name, Creator, doesn't mean He is creative. It means He is in charge of creation. He existed before creation. He is eternal, infinite, everlasting, sovereign, and chief. Like an artist who controls every brushstroke, so our God creates the masterpiece of creation. Even our own bodies and the way He designed them proclaim His majesty.

Job 38–40 are my favorite chapters to find the greatness of God in creation. Job questions God in his suffering, and God responds by reminding Job that He is the majestic Creator. God's answer reminds us of His place as the One who laid the foundations of the earth, tells the oceans where to stop, commands time, and tells the sun when to rise. When God finishes, Job responds, *"Behold, I am of small account; what shall I answer you? I lay my hand on my mouth"* (Job 40:4). I am so small. He is so great. He alone is worthy.

Yes, sin marred our world. Sin brought brokenness into *this* place, but it could not overcome the majesty and the glory of our great God. And in *this* place, God brought hope through Jesus. Because God is faithfully worthy, we can praise Him even in *this* place.

EXTRA VERSES FOR STUDY OR PRAYER

Job 38–40; Romans 11:33–36

VERSE OF THE DAY

O LORD, our Lord, how majestic is your name in all the earth!
—Psalm 8:9

PRAYER

God, You are majestic in *this* place. You alone are worthy in *this* place. Though my eyes are wet with tears, and my heart is wrestling with pain, You are faithfully worthy. Who can be Your counselor? Who can compare to Your majesty? Let my heart sing Your praise. Let my lips tell of Your greatness. Even in *this* place, Lord, I worship You.

THINK

_____

_____

_____

PRAY

_____

_____

_____

PRAISE

_____

_____

_____

TO-DO

PRAYER LIST

QUESTIONS FOR DEEPER REFLECTION

1. What is *this* place for you right now?

---

2. How can you magnify God's great name even here?

DAY 29

FAITHFULLY SET
YOUR MIND ON CHRIST

If then you have been raised with Christ, seek the things that are above, where Christ is, seated at the right hand of God. Set your minds on things that are above, not on things that are on earth. For you have died, and your life is hidden with Christ in God.
—Colossians 3:1–3

I cannot imagine what the sound must have been like. There were millions of Israelites stuck between the harsh wilderness and the Red Sea. I imagine there was a low rumble of murmuring as they awaited their next step. And then, all of a sudden, the sound of hundreds of chariots shook the desert. Pharaoh's men were rapidly approaching, and the Israelites shifted their gaze.

When Pharaoh drew near, the people of Israel lifted up their eyes, and behold, the Egyptians were marching after them, and they feared greatly. Exodus 14:10

Where we look matters. In Exodus 14:1–2, God had given specific instructions on which direction the Israelites were to face. He told them to face forward because God was in a pillar of cloud, leading them through the desert. God was in front of them, but they took their eyes off God and locked eyes on their enemy. Fear ensued.

What we set our minds on matters. God's ways are not our ways, and His thoughts are not our thoughts. (See Isaiah 55:8–9.) The call throughout Scripture is for us to shift our minds toward the things of God instead of the things of man because we no longer belong to this world. We have died to our old selves and are raised to new life in Jesus.

Here's where I'm wrestling with this: I'm learning that the things of God are more about eternity and who we are becoming during our time on earth, and less about what job I have, which house I live in, my earthly healing, or satisfying the desires of my sinful flesh. God wants our whole hearts. He wants our full devotion. He wants our full focus. Not because He is selfish or thinks He is so much better, but because He knows what awaits us when we faithfully look to Him.

"Let the word of Christ dwell in you richly" (Colossians 3:16) as you put to death the propensity toward sin and flesh and continue to keep your focus on the things above.

SOMETHING TO THINK ABOUT

What does it look like to set our minds on Jesus? Scripture gives us several ways we can do this and identifies the benefits we experience when we do. Here are just a few:

+ Setting our minds on Jesus allows us to discern the will of God. (See Romans 12:1–2.) When we seek God and allow our minds to be transformed, no longer conforming to the world, we are better able to discern God's will. This doesn't necessarily mean we will know what we should do, but that we are becoming more like Christ.

+ Setting our minds on Jesus allows us to experience God's peace. (See Philippians 4:8–9.) Paul gives us guidelines to discern what are the things of God. In the moments we question our thoughts, we can ask: Is this true? Is this honorable? Is this pure? If not, it's not of God. When we do shift and set our minds on Him, He promises His peace in our lives.

+ Setting our minds on Jesus keeps us from drifting. (See Hebrews 2:1.) When we take our eyes off God and lock them on our enemy, we will drift. There's no other option. The Greek word used for *pay attention* means "to turn the mind to." We do not drift toward closeness; we drift away from God. Fixing our eyes on Him will not happen naturally. We must intentionally turn our minds to God, and we must faithfully keep doing it day by day, moment by moment, or we will drift toward the world.

Where you look matters. What you set your mind on matters. Faithfully look to Jesus and set your mind on Him.

EXTRA VERSES FOR STUDY OR PRAYER

Isaiah 55:8–9; Mark 8:31–38; Philippians 4:8–9; Hebrews 2:1

VERSE OF THE DAY

If then you have been raised with Christ, seek the things that are above, where Christ is, seated at the right hand of God. Set your minds on things that are above, not on things that are on earth. For you have died, and your life is hidden with Christ in God.
—Colossians 3:1–3

PRAYER

Lord, Your thoughts are not my thoughts, and Your ways are not my ways. Help me turn my mind to the things of You—things that are true, honorable, just, pure, lovely, commendable, excellent, and praiseworthy. I long to be transformed by the renewing of my mind, not locking eyes on my enemy and being filled with fear. Instead, may I continue to lock eyes on You and feel Your promised peace.

THINK

PRAY

_____

_____

_____

PRAISE

_____

_____

_____

TO-DO   PRAYER LIST

_____   _____

_____   _____

_____   _____

QUESTIONS FOR DEEPER REFLECTION

1. In what areas have you allowed yourself to focus on the
    world instead of on God?

_____

_____

2. How can you pay much closer attention to God and faith-
    fully keep your eyes fixed on Jesus?

_____

_____

_____

DAY 30

GOD IS FAITHFUL
TO RETURN

And I heard a loud voice from the throne saying, "Behold, the
dwelling place of God is with man. He will dwell with them, and
they will be his people, and God himself will be with them as their
God. He will wipe away every tear from their eyes, and death
shall be no more, neither shall there be mourning, nor crying, nor
pain anymore, for the former things have passed away."
—Revelation 21:3 4

"Hurting makes us hunger for heaven." As I sat in a conference and heard Whitney Capps utter those words, tears welled up in my eyes. It's so true. The last several years of my life have been marked by hurting. Without a doubt, I can say that I long for heaven like I never have before. I long for the day when our bodies are whole and function as they should. I long for the day when our lips are filled with God's praise, and our words are filled with kindness toward one another. I long for the day when fear no longer grips us and peace prevails. I long for the day when tears are no more, and eternal joy is at our right hand. I long for that day—and it will come.

The story of God's faithfulness throughout all of Scripture proves to us that He will do as He says He will. And that means He will be faithful to return.

And while they were gazing into heaven as he went, behold, two
men stood by them in white robes, and said, "Men of Galilee,

why do you stand looking into heaven? This Jesus, who was taken
up from you into heaven, will come in the same way as you saw
him go into heaven."   Acts 1:10–11

This life in between is not easy, and most days, I wish He would
hurry up. But our Lord is eternal and beyond time. While it may feel
like He is slow in fulfilling this promise to us, He is not. He is delib-
erate in His timing, and one day, He will come.

But do not overlook this one fact, beloved, that with the Lord one
day is as a thousand years, and a thousand years as one day. The
Lord is not slow to fulfill his promise as some count slowness, but
is patient toward you, not wishing that any should perish, but
that all should reach repentance. But the day of the Lord will
come like a thief.   2 Peter 3:8–10

One glorious day, He will come for us, and when He does, He
will make all things new.

SOMETHING TO THINK ABOUT

Revelation 21 gives us the picture of what is coming, and I want
you to read it in its entirety. I cannot say it any better.

Then I saw a new heaven and a new earth, for the first heaven
and the first earth had passed away, and the sea was no more.
And I saw the holy city, new Jerusalem, coming down out of
heaven from God, prepared as a bride adorned for her husband.
And I heard a loud voice from the throne saying, "Behold, the
dwelling place of God is with man. He will dwell with them, and
they will be his people, and God himself will be with them as their
God. He will wipe away every tear from their eyes, and death
shall be no more, neither shall there be mourning, nor crying,
nor pain anymore, for the former things have passed away." And
he who was seated on the throne said, "Behold, I am making all
things new." Also he said, "Write this down, for these words are
trustworthy and true." And he said to me, "It is done! I am the

Alpha and the Omega, the beginning and the end."

Revelation 21:1–6

Tears fill my eyes every time I read those words. What a glorious day that will be. The Alpha and the Omega, the beginning and the end, the One who is eternal, before all things, Creator of all the earth, will make *all things new.* He will dwell with us, and we will dwell with Him. He will be our God, and we will be His people. There shall be no more weeping or mourning. We will live in full faith, full assurance, full trust.

He is coming back, sweet sister. Until that day, let's move forward in faith. Let's proclaim His faithfulness.

Let us hold fast the confession of our hope without wavering, for he who promised is faithful. And let us consider how to stir up one another to love and good works, not neglecting to meet together, as is the habit of some, but encouraging one another, and all the more as you see the Day drawing near.

Hebrews 10:23–25

He will be faithful to return. This is trustworthy and true.

EXTRA VERSES FOR STUDY OR PRAYER

John 14:1–4; Acts 1:6–11; Hebrews 10:23–25

VERSE OF THE DAY

And I heard a loud voice from the throne saying, "Behold, the dwelling place of God is with man. He will dwell with them, and they will be his people, and God himself will be with them as their God. He will wipe away every tear from their eyes, and death shall be no more, neither shall there be mourning, nor crying, nor pain anymore, for the former things have passed away."

—Revelation 21:3–4

PRAYER

Jesus, You have been faithful, and You will be faithful forevermore. I know that You are coming back, and in You, all things will be made new. As I await that day, Lord, help me hold fast to my faith. Let me remember that Your words are trustworthy and true, and I can put my full faith in them. Come, Lord Jesus. Come.

THINK

_____

_____

_____

PRAY

_____

_____

_____

PRAISE

_____

_____

_____

TO-DO

_____

_____

_____

PRAYER LIST

_____

_____

_____

QUESTIONS FOR DEEPER REFLECTION

1. What makes you long for heaven?

2. As you wait, how can you hold fast and encourage your sisters as we are called to in Hebrews 10:23–25?

APPENDIX:
THE PLAN OF SALVATION

But now the righteousness of God has been manifested apart from the law, although the Law and the Prophets bear witness to it—the righteousness of God through faith in Jesus Christ for all who believe. For there is no distinction: for all have sinned and fall short of the glory of God, and are justified by his grace as a gift, through the redemption that is in Christ Jesus, whom God put forward as a propitiation by his blood, to be received by faith. This was to show God's righteousness, because in his divine forbearance he had passed over former sins. It was to show his righteousness at the present time, so that he might be just and the justifier of the one who has faith in Jesus.
—Romans 3:21–26

The entire gospel is summed up in these verses from Romans.

Recognize our sin and need for a Savior:

+ There is a standard of law required to stand in the presence of God.

+ We have all sinned and cannot live up to the standard required for living in God's presence.

+ We need a Savior.

Recognize that faith in Jesus is the only way:

+ The Old Testament points us to Jesus.

+ We are only justified because of the sacrifice of Jesus.
+ We cannot earn our salvation through good works; it is only a gift from God.
+ We are saved by faith alone.

Because of the blood of Jesus, we are justified and made righteous, and we respond in light of these truths.

> *Because, if you confess with your mouth that Jesus is Lord and believe in your heart that God raised him from the dead, you will be saved. For with the heart one believes and is justified, and with the mouth one confesses and is saved.*   Romans 10:9–10

Confess your sin before God, put your whole faith in Him, and surrender your will for His will. You are saved, given the gift of eternal life, and you now get to experience a life-giving relationship with God.

A PRAYER OF SALVATION

Jesus, thank You for coming and doing what we could not. You paid the price so that I might be saved, not just from hell, but for relationship with You. I believe in You, Lord Jesus. I confess that I am a sinner in desperate need of Your grace. Please save me. I give You my life and surrender to Your ways. Thank You for being faithful to save those who call on You.

NOW WHAT?

Welcome to the family of God! I encourage you to talk with a friend or pastor and let them know you've given your life to Jesus. They can help get you connected with a mentor or small group Bible study that will help you learn more about what it means to follow Jesus.

ABOUT THE AUTHOR

Erin H. Warren is passionate about equipping and encouraging women to discover God's truths for themselves. She is the author of *Feasting on Truth: Savor the Life-Giving Word of God* as well as several Bible study books.

Erin leads and teaches Bible study through her ministry Feasting on Truth. She is also a freelance video producer, editor, and designer through Headley Warren Productions LLC.

A graduate of the University of Central Florida with a B.A. in Radio/TV, Erin has served and worked in local church women's ministry for years. She also worked as a producer for the Golf Channel.

Erin loves to cook and hopes tacos never go out of style. She and her husband Kris have two boys and a girl.

To connect with Erin, visit:

erinhwarren.com

FeastingOnTruth.com

www.youtube.com/c/erinhwarren

Instagram: @erinhwarren or @feastingontruth